There are three things
That hold my heart Loves' captive
My fair Inés, cured ham,
And aubergines and cheese

Baltasar de Alcázar

This menu reader is a handy dictionary of Spanish words and terms connected with food found in restaurants throughout Spain and Latin America, its size makes it very easy to carry and use at the restaurant table.

The book is divided into three sections Spanish-English, English-Spanish and Self Catering and Shopping. It's principles are quite simple:-

a) items are arranged in strict alphabetical order

b) there are no capital letters for proper nouns eg catalan, valencia, etc

c) on every occasion prefixes such as *en*, *de* and *a la* are ignored eg to find *la vasca* look up *vasca (a la)*

d) on many occasions the same word can have more than one definition - often it depends on regional variations eg salmorejo has a choice of 5 alternatives

e) cheeses are listed under their individual names eg to find queso de cadiz, look up cadiz

f) symbols are used to denote dishes/terms not generally found in mainland Spain

(Mex) Mexico	(LA) Latin America
(USA) United States	(CA) Central America
of America	(SA) South America

g) the non-Spanish speaker can point to the particular dish or phrase required

Since there are so many regional variations in Spanish cuisine I hope you can appreciate that no work of this size could ever be considered complete. Any contributions readers may find on their travels would be gratefully received for inclusion in future editions. I hope this book goes some way towards helping you to both enjoy and be more adventurous when ordering Spanish food.

¡buen provecho!

Maggie Plunkett
Stanway Publications
West Linden Lodge
Colwall, Malvern, Worcs.

© Stanway Publications
January 2000

First Published in UK 1999
by Stanway Publications

Copyright © Maggie Plunkett
Stanway Publications

ISBN 0953285 812

A

a fuega el pitu	a dry, pungent, cone-shaped cheese
a la sal	fish / poultry encrusted in coarse salt and baked
abadejo	pollack (fish)
abajá de pescado	a fish stew - a speciality from cadiz
abajao	wild asparagus soup
abanda	separate/apart
acecinado	cured / salted
acedera	sorrel
acedía	dab / minature sole (traditionally fried)
aceite	oil
aceite de cártamo	safflower oil
aceite de girasol	sunflower oil
aceite de semillas	mixed cooking oils (not soy or olive)
aceitoso	oily / greasy
aceitunas	olives
acelga	swiss chard
acelga a la malagueña	chard cooked with raisins
acelgas	wild spinach
acerolas	wild fruits
achicoria	endive / chicory (USA)
acuoso	juicy
aderezado	seasoned
aderezo (de ensalada)	seasoning (dressing)
adobo	i) batter, used in deep frying
	ii) a marinade of vinegar, wine, salt, chilli, garlic, lemon and spices - a mexican speciality
adobo (a la madrileña)	meat marinade consisting of garlic, paprika, wine and vinegar
afrutado	fruited
afumados	assorted smoked meats
agachadiza	snipe
agarroso	sour tart (C Am)
agrio	sour
agrura	sourness, tartness
agua	water
agua de azahar	orange blossom water
agua de grifo	tap water
agua dulce	fresh water
agua mineral	mineral water

agua potable	drinking water
agua purificada	bottled water
aguacate	avocado
aguacate con gambas	prawn and avocado cocktail
aguardiente (de caña)	clear liquor, brandy (rum)
aguaturma	jerusalem artichoke
aguja	i) chuck steak
	ii) gar, needle fish
	iii) sweet pastry (used in meat pies)
ahumado	smoked
ajetes	garlic shoots
ajiaceite	garlic mayonnaise
ajillo	a sauce of fried cloves and garlic in olive oil with a little chilli pepper - usually served as a fish accompaniment
ajo	garlic
ajo arriero	i) grilled cod cooked with pepper, garlic, onion and tomato
	ii) a cod and salt paste served with toasted bread
ajo blanco	a cold soup, similar to gazpacho, with almonds and garlic ground in oil with water added, grapes can also be included - a malaga speciality
ajo colorado	a red pepper, garlic, potato and onion purée
ajo pollo	potato chunks cooked with a sauce of spices, garlic, almonds and fried bread - sometimes shellfish or fish are also added during the last 10 minutes of cooking
ajoaceite	an oil and garlic sauce, can be served with meat, poultry, fish, eggs or vegetables
ajoharina de jaen	potatoes stewed with peppers and garlic
ajonjolí	sesame seed
ajos tiernos	young garlic
al ajillo	in garlic
alaju	a sweet made from honey, almonds, breadcrumbs and orange water
alaravea	caraway seed
alas	wings (chicken)
albacora	long fin tunny / small tuna (whiter meat than tuna)
albahaca	basil
albaricoque	apricot

albariño	i) a galician white wine / grape
	ii) stewed summer vegetables
albóndigas	spiced meatballs
albóndigas de ternera	veal meatballs
albondigon de ternera	veal meatballs
albondiguilla	faggot
alboronia	stewed summer vegetables, similar to ratatouille, flavoured with honey, saffron and aniseed - a speciality from la mancha
alborotos	popcorn
alcachofas	artichokes
alcachofas aliñadas	marinaded pork loin with artichokes
alcachofas y patatas	an artichoke heart and potato purée - served as a garnish for fried brains
alcaparras	capers
alcaravea	caraway (seeds)
alcuzcuz	couscous
alfajores	almond and cinnamon sweetmeats
alfalfa	alfalfa sprouts
alfeñique	almond flavoured sugar pastry
alga(s)	seaweed / kelp
algarroba	carob bean
alicante	soft white goats' cheese
alimentos infantiles	baby food
aliñada	marinaded
aliño	i) seasoning / dressing / marinade (anything in a vinegar and oil dressing)
	ii) parsley, chopped garlic and lemon - accompaniment for grilled fish
alioli	garlic mayonnaise
alitán	member of the shark family
all cremat	well-cooked garlic - a toasted taste
all i oli	olive oil and garlic sauce - garlic mayonnaise
all i pebre	garlic, olive oil and paprika sauce, most popularly served with fish dishes
almejas	clams
almejas a la marinera	clams cooked with an oil, garlic, wine and parsley sauce
almendra	almond
almendrados de castellón	almond macaroons
almendra garapiñada	sugar coated almond

almíbar	syrup
almilla	breast of pork
almuerzo	late breakfast
alondra	lark
alubias	white beans
amanida	catalan salad, consisting of escarole sausage, celery, onions and anchovies - tossed with a garlic mayonnaise
amb	with
anacardos	cashews
anaheim	large, mild fresh chilli
anca	haunch
ancas de rana	frogs' legs
ancho	type of dried chilli - large and leathery
anchoas	anchovies (salted)
anec amb figues	duck cooked with figs
anec amb peres	roast duck cooked with pears
anec amb peres i nabos	braised baby turnips and pears with duck
anehoas	anchovies
añejo	ripe
anguila (ahumada)	(smoked) eel
anguila (de mar)	eel (conger)
anguila al all i pebre	eel stew - a valencian speciality
angulas	thin, spaghetti-like baby eels
anillas	rings
anís	i) anisette (liqueur)
	ii) aniseed
añojo	beef (yearling)
añojo (becerro) (cordero)	yearling (calf) (lamb)
ánsar á común	goose (greylag)
ansó	a pyrenean sheep's milk cheese with a creamy, white appearance and texture
antojitos	starters
aperitivos	apéritifs
api	boiled maize, wheat or rice
apio	celery
apio nabo	celeriac
araña	weever (fish)
arándanos	blueberries
arasá	guava (LA)
arbitán	ling, similar to whiting (fish)
arbol	dried chilli - very hot
arenque	herring

arenque ahumado	bloater
arete	red gurnard
armada	semi-hard cheese, sharp and slightly bitter - will keep for two or three years
armado	fish - similar to gurnard
arrayán	myrtle
arrope	boiled grape syrup
arros amb crosta	rice cooked with sausage, tomato, pork; various meats, garbanzos and saffron: eggs are added to the casserole and browned in the oven
arros negre amb all i oli	a paella of squid and black rice, tomatoes with a garlic sauce - a catalan speciality
arroz	rice
arroz a la catalana	saffron rice with squid, spicy pork, sausages, tomato, peas and chilli pepper
arroz a la cubana	a dish of white rice, banana, fried eggs and a savoury tomato sauce
arroz abanda	a rice dish of all types of seafood, tomato, potatoes and onions. The fish and potatoes are often removed and served as a first course, followed by the rice and a garlic sauce
arroz amb fessols i naps	a rice, beans and turnip dish – pigs' ears, trotters and black pudding can be added
arroz azafranado	saffron rice
arroz bomba	short grain rice
arroz con leche	rice pudding
arroz con leche planchado	
	sticky sweet, aromatic rice topped with caramelised sugar
arroz empedrado	a valencian dish of tomatoes and cod layered with white beans
arroz integral	brown rice
arroz murciano	rice with pork, red peppers, tomatoes and saffron
arroz navarro	rice and lamb casserole, baked with tomato sauce
arroz negro	a squid, garlic, tomato and rice dish. The rice is coloured black by cooking in squid ink
arroz rosetxat	rice and lamb casserole
arroz santanderino	rice with salmon and milk
asadillo	roasted red peppers, served with a tomato, oil and garlic dressing
asado	baked/roasted
asado a la parilla	grilled

asador	a large charcoal grill
asaduras	offal/giblets (bird)
asadurilla de cordero	lamb's liver
atascaburros	rabbit casseroled with onion, garlic, tomatoes, wine, cognac and spices
atole	a ground corn, sugar and water drink (Mex)
atún	tuna / tunny fish
atún encebollado	oven-baked layers of tomatoes, garlic, parsley, chopped walnuts, tuna fillets and red peppers - dish surrounded by fried potatoes
atún fresco a la bilbainita	tunny (tuna) fish baked in a tomato sauceand covered with garlic and bread-crumbs - traditionally served with diced, boiled potatoes, garlic and parsley
aubilete	custard mould
avellanas	hazelnuts / filberts
avena	oats
aves	poultry
avestruz	ostrich
ayocote	kidney bean
ayote	pumpkin
azafrán	saffron
azahar	orange blossom
azúcar (moreno)	(brown) sugar
azúcar quemado	caramel
azúcar tamizado / de lustre	icing sugar

B

bacaladilla	blue whiting (fish)
bacalao	(salt) cod
bacalao a la manchega	salt cod cooked with anise brandy
bacalao a la riojana	oven-baked layers of salt cod, fried onion, sweet paprika and strips of red pepper
bacalao a la vizcaina	oven-baked salt cod with a salsa española, chillies, garlic and fried bread. Strips of red peppers, parsley and breadcrumbs are added to the final layer
bacalao al ajo arriero	a salt cod, eggs and garlic – a castile-león dish

bacalao al pil-pil	i) cod fried with garlic and oil and set in a green sauce made from the gelatine of the fish (can be spicy)
	ii) salt cod, garlic and parsley simmered with olive oil in a casserole
bacalao con patatas	fried salt cod served with sliced, boiled potatoes, onions and parsley
bacalao desalado	desalted cod
bacalao monocal	cod cooked with spinach and potatoes
bagre	catfish
baila	fish similar to sea bass
bajoques farcidas	peppers stuffed with rice, pork, tomatoes and spices
balarrasa	strong brandy
bandeja de fiambres	assorted cold meats
banderillas	small savoury snacks (e.g. gherkins, red peppers, silver onions and tidbits), on a cocktail stick or skewer - served as tapas
barbacoa	barbecue
barbo	barbel (fish)
barbo de mar	red mullet
barcos	hollowed out pastry / cucumber - stuffed with a variety of fillings
barcos de jamón	little tapa-sized pasties filled with ham, pickles, olives and mayonnaise
bardana	burdock
barnada	goose
barra	loaf of bread, baguette
barril (de)	draught
basilico	basil
batata (camote)	sweet potato (yam)
batidos	shakes
baya	berry
baya del saúco	elderberry
bebidas	drinks
becada	woodcock
beef steack	steak
béicon	bacon
bejel	tub gurnard (fish)
bellota	acorn
berberecho	cockle
berenjena	aubergine / eggplant (USA)

berenjena a la catalana	cubes of aubergine (egg plant (USA)) fried with walnuts or hazelnuts and casseroled with onion, garlic and tomatoes until tender
berenjena a la romano	
	batter-fried aubergine (egg plant (USA))
berenjena arcense	spicy aubergine (egg plant (USA)) with ham and chorizo
berenjena catalina	baked moulds of aubergine (egg plant (USA)) strips, red (bell (USA)) pepper and parsley - served with a white wine sauce of onions, tomatoes, ham and mushrooms
berro	cress
berro(s) de agua	watercress
berza	cabbage
berza a la andaluza	an andalusian vegetable hotpot
berza lombarda	red cabbage
besito	coconut bun
besugo	(sea) bream / porgy (USA)
besugo a la donostiarra	
	bream grilled on a charcoal fire
besugo a la espalda	red bream split and grilled over coals
besugo a la madrileña	
	red sea-bream, marinaded in lemon juice and baked with lemons and wine
besugo al horno	baked red bream
besuguera	shallow oval fish pan
beyusco	a mixed ewes' and goats' milk cheese with a pleasant aroma and slightly sharp flavour - it has a hard amber skin if aged, or soft and creamy if fresh - lightly smoked
bien asado	well done (meat)
bien cocido	well done (meat)
bien hecho	well done (meat)
bien pasado	well done
bife (a caballo)	beef steak (with two fried eggs)
bígaro	winkle
birria	tender, barbecued or pot roasted meat
bitokes	patties of beef - similar to a hamburger
bizcochá manchega	a sponge cake soaked in milk, sugar, vanilla and cinnamon
bizcocho	pound cake
bizcochos borrachos	cakes soaked in liqueur

blanco	white
blando	soft
blanquillo	egg (Mex)
bocadillo	sandwich or french bread (with various fillings)
bocarte	anchovy
bocata	sandwich
bodio	variety of wrasse (fish)
boga	small bream
bogavante	black / green lobster
bogavente a la gallega	lobster meat cooked with onion, garlic and tomatoes in a white wine, paprika sauce
bola de mas hervida	dumpling
boleto	boletus mushroom
bolets am pernil	large red pine mushrooms cooked with ham and parsley in a sherry sauce
boletus	a variety of wild mushroom usually sautéed with fresh herbs and a hint of garlic
bolillo	french roll (Mex)
bolinchos de bacalao	deep-fried cod fish and potato balls
bollo	i) bread roll
	ii) sweet danish roll
bombana (de vino)	carafe (of wine)
bombón de chocolate y caramelo	chocolate éclair
boniato	sweet potato / yam
bonito	striped tunny (tuna)
bonito a la bilbaina	thick slices of tuna (tunny fish) boiled in stock, bones removed and served with a hard-boiled egg, onion, parsley and pickle relish
boquerones fritos	small anchovies, deep fried
boquerones al natural	marinaded fresh anchovies
boquerones huecos	anchovies fried in fluffy golden batter
borona	maize / corn (Am)
borracho	i) grey gurnard
	ii) rum baba
borrachos	small squares of sponge cake drizzled with wine syrup and dusted with cinnamon - 'drunken' cakes
borrachuelos	doughnut - rolls with a slight aniseed, sesame seed and wine flavour
borraja	borage
borrego(a)	yearling lamb

botella	bottle
botellín	a small bottle of beer
botifarra	white pork sausage
brasa (a la)	char-grilled
braseada	braised
brázo de gitano	cake filled with custard cream, rolled and topped with the remaining cream, literally 'gypsy's arm'
breca	small red sea bream
brecol	broccoli
brema	bream
brevas	blue figs
brioche danés	danish pastry
brocheta	skewer / kebab
broculi	broccoli
brote	bean sprout
brótola	forkbread (fish), similar to whiting
bruno	black plum
brut	dry sparkling wine
bruto	extra-dry
budín	pudding
budín relleno	dumpling
buccino	whelk
buey	i) ox
	ii) beef from older animal
	iii) type of crab
bufe (libre)	(self-service) buffet
bullabesa	bouillabaisse
bullevesa mallorquina	
	a fish soup, similar to bouillabaisse
buñuelitos	small fritters made with ham, fish, egg or a wide variety of other fillings
buñuelos	fried dough with sugar and honey (Mex)
buñuelos de bacalao	deep-fried cod fish and potato-cakes
buñuelos de batata	sweet potato fritters
buñuelos de queso	cheese puffs
buñuelos de viento	lightweight fritters; usually filled with cream or jam
bunyols	catalan dish of fried pastries
burgos	sausages

burgos (queso de) a round creamy, soft cheese made with a mixture of cow, goat and sheep's milk, similar to mozzarella - the fresh cheeses are steeped in brine for 24 hours - resulting in a salty flavour. Often served with honey and walnuts as dessert

burrida de ratjada boiled skate / ray with a ground almond, garlic and egg sauce

búsano whelk

butifarra (blanca) medium to coarse, mildly seasoned (white) pork sausage - a catalan speciality

butifarra dolca sugar-cured pork sausage, resulting in a sweet taste

butifarra negra medium to coarse, slightly fatty, mildy seasoned, dark blood sausage

C

caballa (al horno) mackerel (baked)

cabello de ángel sweet made of syrup and gourd

cabeza head

cabra i) goat
ii) rascasse (fish)

cabracho (al ajillo) scorpion fish / rascasse (cooked with garlic)

cabrales a round strong, tangy, veined goat cheese from asturias, similar to roquefort

cabraliego a strong, tangy, veined cheese from asturias - originally made from cows' milk and aged in mountain caves, this cheese, which resembles roquefort in taste, is now produced industrially and is generally made from mixed sheeps', cows' and goats' milk. The skin is dark grey and is encased in leaves

cabrilla similar to grouper fish / rockfish (Mex)

cabrito baby goat / kid

cacahuazintle corn with a very large white kernel / hominy (USA)

cacahuetas peanuts

caça wild game

cacerola casserole

cachelada gallega octopus casserole

cachelada leonesa sausage (chorizo) and potato casserole

cachelos jacket potatoes

cachelos con jamón	a spicy dish of red potatoes and boiled ham - a speciality from the guadarrama mountains
cachorreña	bitter orange
cachorreñas	fish soup cooked with orange peel
cadera	round (rump) steak (USA) / sirloin (beef)
cadiz	a goats' cheese, white and full of small holes - a strong but pleasant flavour
café	coffee
café cargado	strong coffee
café con crema	coffee with cream
café con leche	white coffee
café cortado	small black coffee with a little milk
café descafeinado	decaffeinated coffee
café doble	large cup of white coffee
café expresso	black espresso coffee (Mex)
café exprés	espresso coffee
café grande	large cup of white coffee
café negro/con leche	black/white coffee
café solo	i) black coffee
	ii) black (espresso)
café sombra	very milky coffee
café torrefacto	high roast coffee
cailón	porbeagle shark
cailón en amarillo	shark cooked in saffron
cajeta	i) sweet
	ii) biscuit
	iii) fruit custard (Mex)
calabaciatas	courgettes (Mex)
calabacín	courgette / zucchini (USA)
calabaza	pumpkin, squash
calamacets	tiny squid
calamares	squid
calamares a la romana	squid deep-fried in butter
calapé	roast tortoise or turtle
calçotada	fresh sweet onions, roasted and served with an olive oil and almond sauce
calçotada con romesco y alioli	grilled spring onions, served with a garlic sauce
calçotada de valls	grilled / barbecued spring onions served with alioli or romesco sauce
calcots	bulbous sweet spring onions
caldeirada	a dish of potatoes and fish - a sofrito of garlic, onion, paprika, olive oil and vinegar is added before serving

calderata	pieces of goat meat fried and cooked with peppers (piquante) and seasoned with garlic, red peppers and minced liver
calderata asturiana	layers of mixed fish and seafood with parsley and onions, casseroled in a pimento, herbs, sherry and white wine sauce
calderata de cordero	lamb casseroled with onions, tomatoes, peppers and spices
calderata de langosta/ de llagosta	pieces of lobster cooked with pepper, onion, tomato, garlic and herb liqueur
calderata extremeña	a lamb or kid goat stew
caldereta	a thick fish stew - speciality of asturias
caldereta asturiana	a fish and seafood stew layered with onions and pepper purée - pepper, nutmeg, cayenne and sherry are added before cooking
calderete de cordero	lamb casseroled slowly with onions, garlic and green peppers - potatoes added later
caldero al estilo de mar menor	a fish stew, consisting of whiting and grey mullet, sea spider, onion and chilli peppers
caldillo	spicy minced meat stew
caldo	stock / broth
caldo de gallina	chicken stock
caldo gallego	a dish of ham, chorizo, spare ribs, cabbage, gammon, potatoes, haricot beans, and spinach or turnip tops - a galician speciality
caldo michi	a mexican fish soup
caldo tlalpeno	a chicken and avocado soup - garlic / chilli is often added - a speciality from mexico
caliente	hot (temperature)
calimocho	drink made with wine and coca cola
callos	tripe, normally cooked in a hot paprika sauce
callos a la andaluza	similar to madrid dish of tripe but with garbanzos and mint added
callos a la extremeña	tripe cooked with black pudding (blood sausage (USA)) and lamb's feet
callos a la madrileña	a spicy casserole of tripe, pigs foot, ham, wine, onions, black pudding (blood sausage (USA)), paprika, thyme and chilli pepper - chorizo can also be added

callos a la riojana	tripe cooked with wine - a speciality from the rioja area
camarones grandes	prawns
camarón	small prawn / shrimp
camerano	a riojan speciality - a fresh goat cheese shaped into a ball with a pleasant lightly acidic taste
camerero / camerera	waiter / waitress
campechana	oval-shaped puff pastry with a caramelised top
campechano	mixture of spirits (drink (Mex))
campero	a sandwich, served hot or cold, with cooked ham, tomato, cheese, lettuce and mayonnaise
canagroc	a bright yellow, long and slender wild mushroom with a little brown top
canas	ingredients of dish soaked in milk
canasta / cestilla del pan	
	bread basket
caña	i) pork loin
	ii) glass of beer
caña de lomo	pork loin (tapa)
caña fritas	cream-filled pastry
candeal	drink made of milk, eggs and brandy (LA)
canela	cinnamon
canelones	cannelonni
cangrejo (de mar)	freshwater crab
cangrejo (de río)	freshwater crayfish
cantina	similar to an english pub or american tavern
canuto	tube-shaped sorbet
cap roig	scorpion fish, redfish, red snapper or rascasse cooked whole and served with a sautéed garlic, oil and chopped parsley sauce
capa (de chocolate)	coating (of chocolate)
capia	maize / corn
capirotada	a meat, vegetables and cheese dish
capitón	grey mullet
capón (mallorquin)	capon (stuffed with black cherries, apple, raisins, pine kernels and sherry - a majorcan speciality)
caqui	persimmon
carabineros	large, deep red-orange shrimps
caracol (es)	snail(s)
caracol de mar	periwinkle

caracola	sea snail
carajillo	coffee with a dash of brandy
carapacho	seafood dish cooked in the shell
carbonera	a variety of wild mushroom
carbonero	coley / coalfish
cardamomo	cardamom
cardos	cardoons (a cross between celery and an artichoke)
cargolins	snails
cari	curry powder
carne	meat
carne de agujas	shoulder (meat)
carne de buey	beef
carne de cerdo (adobada)	pork (brawn)
carne de cordero	lamb
carne de lidia	beef from fighting bulls
carne de membrillo	quince jelly
carne de monte	'mountain meat' - venison or wild boar
carne de res	beef
carne de ternera	veal
carne de vaca rellena	thin slices of beef flattened, filled with a stuffing of olives, hard boiled eggs, red pepper, spinach and garlic then rolled and braised
carne de vacuno	beef
carne molida	minced meat
carne molida cruda	raw, coarsely minced steak mixed with pepper, chillies and onion - lime juice is added to tenderise the meat
carne picada	minced meat / ground meat
carne vacuna	beef
carnero	mutton
carpa	carp
carpaccio	marinaded raw meat or fish
carradetas	wild mushrooms
carruécano	pumpkin fried with garlic and chillies
carta	menu
cártamo	safflower
casadielles	fried or baked squares of pastry filled with a ground walnut, sherry and lemon mixture - a galician speciality

cáscara	shell (nut/egg), skin, peel (fruit), husk
caserola	home-made
casi crudo	rare (cooked)
cassolada	a potato and vegetable stew with bacon and ribs
castaña (pilonga)	chestnut (dried)
castañas con leche	chestnut pudding
catalana (a la)	term usually denoting food is served with a tomato and green pepper sauce
cava	type of champagne
cayena	cayenne
caza	game / hunt
cazón	i) dogfish
	ii) tope (fish)
cazón en adobo	marinaded fried fish
cazuela	stew / casserole
cazuela de ave	a rich soup with chicken and green vegetables
cazuela de chivo	baby kid layered with sliced potatoes
cazuela de fideos	a dish of beans, cod, noodles and spices - depending on region, seafood is sometimes included
cazuela de mariscos	seafood stew
cazuela de pescado	mixed fish in a very spicy sauce
cazuela de rape	angler fish baked in a sauce of almonds and pine nuts
cazuelita	small ramekin dish
cebada	barley
cebado	fattened
cebolla	onion
cebollas francesas	tiny, flattish, pink-red onions
cebolleta	chive
cebollino	chive
cebón alqueso de cabrales	venison in a blue-cheese sauce
cebrero	a mushroom-shaped cows' milk cheese with a semi hard skin and smooth in texture - a tangy flavour
cecina	i) salt beef
	ii) thin strips of dried / smoked meats
cena	evening meal / supper
cenouras à la lentejana	sautéed carrots served with a thickened sauce of egg yolk, lemon juice, parsley and beef stock

centeno	rye
centolla / o	spider or spiny crab (small claws, round body and spindly legs)
cerafolio	chervil
cerceta común	teal
cerdo	pig / pork
cerdo agridulce	sweet and sour pork
cerdo rebozado	thin slices of pork covered in egg and breadcrumbs, deep fried and served with fried green peppers
cereales	cereal
cereza	cherry
cervera	an unaged mixture of cows' and sheeps' milk cheese - white and mild in flavour
cerveza	beer
cerveza clara/rubia	light beer
cerveza de barril	draft beer
cerveza de botella	bottled beer
cerveza extranjera	foreign beer
cerveza negra	dark beer (stout)
cestilla / canasta del pan	
	bread basket
ceviche	raw fish, marinaded in lemon juice and served with onions and hot peppers
ceviche de langostinos	
	a mixed shellfish ceviche - crayfish being the main ingredient
chabacano	apricot
chacina	i) smoked / cured meat
	ii) seasoned pork
chacinería	cured meats
chacolí	light, tangy dry white wine from the basque region
chala	maize leaf
chalote	shallot
chalupa	oval-shaped corn-cake
chamberete	shin of beef
champán (andaluz)	champagne (shandy)
champiñon	mushroom (cultivated)
champola	a guanábana fruit drink (C Am / Cuba)
champurrado	chocolate drink (Mex)
chancaca	i) syrup cake
	ii) maize cake with honey

chancaquita	syrup cake with nuts or coconuts
chancho (salvaje)	pork (boar)
chanfaina	i) tender meat stew cooked in red wine (pigs'liver is often used)
	ii) vegetable soup (andalucía)
	iii) similar to a ratatouille - roasted peppers (capsicums (USA)), onions, aubergines (egg plants (USA)), courgettes (zucchini (USA)) and garlic cooked in olive oil until soft
chanfaina a la castellana	
	pigs' liver stew
chanfaina salmantina	a dish from salamanca, comprising of rice, giblets, lamb sweetbreads and pieces of chorizo
changurro	spider or spiny crab - a basque speciality when stuffed
chanquete(s)	i) whitebait
	ii) very young anchovies, deep fried
	iii) miniscule fry of goby fish
charanagua	a mexican drink made from bitter pulque, honey and chilli
charape	a mexican drink of corn, honey, cloves and cinnamon
charcuteriá	i) butcher's shop
	ii) cured pork meats
charqui	i) dried / cured beef (SA)
	ii) dried fruit
charquicán	dried meat and vegetable stew (SA)
chato	a small glass
chayote	pear shaped gourd or squash (Mex)
cherna	stone bass / wreckfish
cherne	firm fleshed white rockfish
chicharo	pea / chickpea
chicharro	scad / horse mackerel
chicharrón	crispy fried pork rind
chicheme	cold drink made of corn milk and sugar (SA)
chilaquiles	strips of tortilla served with an onion, tomato and garlic soup - a mexican dish
chile	chilli
chile cristal	sweet, light, green pepper
chilindrones	a pepper and tomato accompaniment

chilindrón	i) sweet red (bell (USA)) peppers
	ii) an aragon speciality - lamb, chicken or pork braised with onions, peppers, tomatoes and garnished with sweet red pepper strips
	iii) a tomato, onion, garlic, ham and red pepper sauce
chilmole	tomato, onion and pepper sauce (Mex)
chimbo	sweet made from egg yolk, syrup and almonds (LA)
chimichangas	fried rolled flour tortillas (Mex)
china	orange
chipi - chipi	a soup using tiny clams
chipirón	small squid
chipotle	small hot, smoked chilli
chirimoya	cherimoya or custard apple
chirivía	parsnip
chirla	small clam
chistorra	thin spicy sausage cooked over charcoal
chito	fried goat
chivato	kid goat
chivo	kid goat
chocha perdiz	woodcock
choclo	a tender maize stew
choco	small cuttlefish
chocolate (caliente)	(hot) chocolate
chongos	type of caramel custard
chopa	bream
chopitos	tiny squid
choricero	sweet red pepper
chorizo	i) salami, a highly seasoned red coloured pork sausage
	ii) a name given to a large red coloured prawn
chorizo de cantimpalos	
	similar to chorizo de salamanca but the sausages are much smaller
chorizo de pamplona	a finely chopped pork sausage mixed with paprika, spices, herbs and garlic. The sausage is dried for some time and is quite spicy
chorizo de salamanca	a sausage made from large chunks of ham mixed with paprika, garlic, herbs and spices - it is coarser and has a different flavour than chorizo de pamplona
choto (al) ajillo	kid goat braised in wine with garlic

chufa	groundnut
chuleta	chop / cutlet
chuleta de novillo retinto	
	braised young bull cutlets / chops
chuletas al sarmiento	chops cooked over vine wood
chuletas de cerdo a la madrileña	
	pork chops marinaded in garlic, parsley, paprika and thyme then sautéed in oil
chuletas de solomillo	chops including loin and tenderloin
chuleton a la vasca	beef chops grilled with chopped garlic and parsley
chuletón	large beef chop
chumbo	prickly pear
chupe de camarones	a potato, milk, shrimp and hot chillies / peppers soup. Eggs are also added
chupe de mariscos	shellfish stew
chupe de pescado	a fish stew thickened with breadcrumbs
chupito	spirit and mixer combination
churdón	raspberry
churrasco (de cerdo)	grilled / barbecued (pork)
churros	a paste of water, flour, salt and eggs, formed into a sausage shape, deep fried in olive oil and sprinkled with sugar - similar to a crunchy deep-fried doughnut or fritter
cidra	a variety of squash
ciervo (común)	(red) deer
cigala	dublin bay prawn (sea crayfish)
cigarra	'sea cricket' flat lobster
cilantro	coriander
cirecens	a variety of wild mushroom which is most often served marinaded in olive oil and cider vinegar
ciruela	plum
ciruela claudia	greengage
ciruela pasa	prune
cítricos	citrus fruits
civet	stew, ragout
clara	shandy
clavo (de especia)	clove
coca	type of flat cake
coca de trempo	a type of pizza with a pepper, tomato and onion topping

coca mallorquina	a majorcan savoury pizza - fillings can vary e.g. spinach, bacon, peppers, tomatoes, cheese, olives and anchovies
coca valenciana	savoury tart containing tomato and tuna fish
cocas	flat open tarts, similar to pizzas
coccíon	cooking
cochas finas	venus clams
cochifrito	lamb casseroled with onion, garlic, paprika, lemon juice, parsley and wine
cochifrito de cordero	highly seasoned lamb or kid stew
cochifrito navarro	small pieces of deep-fried / sautéed lamb
cochinillo	suckling pig
cochinillo asado	roasted crispy suckling pig (often splayed to cook) - a castillian favourite
cocido	cooked / hotpot or stew
cocido (madrileño)	a chickpea stew, cooked with potatoes, cabbage, turnip, beef, marrow bones, streaky bacon and chorizo and / or black pudding (blood sausage (USA))
cocido (sancocho)	a soup of either chicken, chunks of beef, fish or local vegetables
cocido a fuego lente	braised (meat)
cocido a la sevillana	a stew of fried meat with beaten eggs
cocido al vapor	steamed
cocido castellano	a chickpea, vegetable and meat stew - each served on a separate plate - a castillian favourite
cocido de la casa	a savoury stew of chard, potatoes and chickpeas
cocido español	a stew of meat, pulses (usually chick-peas) and vegetables
cocido madrileño	a hearty chickpea stew cooked with potatoes, cabbage, turnips, beef, marrow bones, streaky bacon, chorizo and / or black pudding and rice - a madrid speciality
cocina	kitchen
cocina casera	home cooking
cocina de mercado	food in season
cocina tipico	local specialities
coco	coconut
cocochas	hake morsels
cóctel	cocktail

cóctel de frutas	fruit cocktail (Mex)
codillo	shoulder (usually of pork)
codornices a la riojana	
	quails inside green peppers casseroled with onions, tomatoes, ham and white wine
codornices con mojo	bacon wrapped quails, casseroled with onion and wine - served with fried potatoes and a wine vinegar, oil and herb dressing
codorniz	quail
cogollitos de tudela	a salad of lettuce hearts in a garlic vinaigrette
cogollo de palmito	palm heart
cogollo(s)	head of lettuce / lettuce hearts
cogote	nape of the neck (fish)
col (blanca)	(white) cabbage
col rizada	kale
cola de pescado	leaf gelatine
colache	a cooked mixture of seasonal vegetables - a mexican speciality
colación	i) light meal / snack
	ii) mixed sweets (Mex)
coles de bruselas	brussel sprouts
coliflor	cauliflower
collá	a type of yoghurt/cheese made with the pistils of wild artichokes
colza	rape seed
comida	lunch
comida corrida	set menu
comida de campo	picnic
comino	cumin (seeds)
compagno	a mixture of morcilla, chorizo and other charcuterie
compota	compote
con hielo	on the rocks (ice)
con sal	with salt
coñac	cognac, brandy
concha	(seafood) shell
concha fina	venus shell clam
concha peregrina	sea scallop
condimentado	seasoned
condimentos	seasoning
conejo	rabbit
conejo a la asturiana	rabbit casseroled in cider with bacon, garlic, turnips, carrots, potatoes and pine nuts

conejo a la bilbaina   a basque speciality - rabbit casseroled with chocolate, parsley, hazelnuts, garlic, herbs and wine

conejo a la cazadora   rabbit in a mushroom and almond sauce

conejo a la navarra   rabbit casseroled with garlic, tomatoes, herbs and wine, potatoes are added later

conejo con maní   rabbit in peanut sauce

conejo con salsa   fried rabbit with an onion, gammon, red wine and chorizo sauce

conejo de monte   wild rabbit

conejo tarraconense   rabbit cooked with onions, tomatoes and red wine and herbs - potatoes and a chilli, saffron, garlic, chocolate and flour mixture is also added later to the casserole

confite   sweet / candy (USA)

confitería   a cake shop

confitura   jam, preserve

congrio   conger eel

conill i pollastre   a rabbit and chicken dish

consomé a la andaluza   a consommé with tomatoes and vermicelli

consomé con yema   piping hot beef consommé with raw egg yolk floating in each bowl

copa   glass

copa de frutas   a fresh fruit salad

copos de maíz   cornflakes

coques   rectangular pastry cases covered with chopped vegetables, minced meat or fish

coques en llanda   spanish pizza

coquetes   a pizza, served with a variety of toppings - pisto, sautéed spinach or chard / tuna chunks, olives and capers

coquina   wedge shell clam

corazón   heart

corcho   cork

corcón   grey mullet

cordero   lamb

cordero a la levantina   lamb casseroled with onions, garlic, tomatoes, herbs, lemon juice and egg yolk - a valencian speciality

cordero asado a la riojana
   lamb basted in white wine and roasted - served with a lamb stock, vinegar, garlic and parsley sauce

cordero con ajo	lamb browned and casseroled with onion, garlic, paprika, vinegar and stock
cordero en chilindrón	sautéed lamb; onion, garlic, peppers and tomatoes casseroled over a low heat (chicken, pork and rabbit also cooked with this method)
cordero lechal	suckling lamb
cordero mozábe	roast lamb with a sweet and sour sauce
cordero verde	lamb casseroled with onions, cured ham or bacon, garlic, orange juice, peas and herbs
coronel	a large glass of house wine
coronillas	almond and cream dessert
cors de carxofes	artichoke hearts
cortado	small coffee with a dash of milk
corteza	zest
corto	small strong coffee
corvina	meagre corb (fish), similar to sea bass
corvina al amontillado	meagre (fish) cooked in dark sherry
corzo	roe deer
costilla	cutlet
costra	crust (pie)
costrada manchega	manchego 'rarebit'
crema	cream / cream soup
crema batida	whipped cream (Mex)
crema catalana	rich custard covered with a sheet of caramelised sugar
crema de aranjuez	cream of asparagus soup
crema de carrerres	cream of mushroom soup
crema de champiñones	cream of mushroom soup
crema quemado (a la catalana)	crème brûlée - a catalan speciality
cremadina	a custard filling for pastry
cremat	usually refers to garlic being very well cooked to bring out its flavour
cremoso	creamy (cheese)
crepe	pancake / crêpe
criadillas	i) sweetbreads
	ii) lamb's testicles deep fried and sliced
criadillas de (la) tierra	i) truffles
	ii) an extremedura speciality - truffles chopped and sautéed with garlic - served with a brown, egg-thickened sauce
crispilla	iceberg lettuce

crizos de mar	sea urchins
crocante	almond brittle
croqueta	rissole
croqueta de pescado	fish-cake
crudo	raw
cuajada	i) mild-flavoured curd cheese with a custard consistency
	ii) a cold cottage cheese dessert layered with sliced fruit on a biscuit base - topped with sugar and cinnamon
cuajo (para queso)	rennet
cuarto trasero	saddle / hindquarter
cuba libre	rum and coke
cuchara	spoon
cuchillo	knife
cuco rubio	gurnard (red)
cucurucho	ice cream cornet
cuerno	croissant
cuerpo (de)	full-bodied
culantro	coriander
cúrcuma	turmeric
curruco	scallops

D

damasco	damson / apricot (LA)
dátil de mar	'sea date' - type of brown mussel
dátiles	dates
delicias de queso (y jamón)	cheese (and ham) savouries
demasiado cruda	too rare
demasiado dura	too tough
demasiado hecha	overdone
dentex	a type of sea bass
dentón	a type of sea bass
desayuno	breakfast
desosado	boned (meat) / stoned (fruit)
despojos	offal, variety of meats
diente de ajo	clove of garlic
diente de león	dandelion
doble	double (a double shot)

doncella	variety of wrasse (fish)
dorado	gilt-head bream
dorado a la sal	a whole bream baked in coarse sea-salt - served with a garlic mayonnaise or a garlic, parsley and oil sauce
draque	drink made of sugar, liquor, water and nutmeg (LA)
dulce	sweet
dulce almíbar	preserved fruit
dulce de batata malagueño	
	a sweet potato pudding - a speciality of malaga
dulce de membrillo	quince jelly
dulce heco con azúcar, leche y mantequilla	fudge
durazno	peach
duro	hard / tough

E

eglefino	haddock
ejote	string bean (CA) (Mex)
elección (a)	of your choice
elote	sweet corn / maize
embuchado	processed cold meat
embutidos	various types of sausages
empañada	crusted pie
empañada de atún	rich, fried pastry stuffed with tuna, egg and onions
empañada de espinacas y queso	spinach and cheese tart
empañada gallega	a savoury tart with a variety of fillings, usually pork, but always contains chorizo, tomatoes and peppers - a galician speciality
empañadas	stuffed savoury pastries
empanadilla	small savoury pasty resembling a cornish pasty but its filling consists of onions, tomatoes, green pepper, smoked haddock and lean ham or fish
empanado	i) pie ii) breaded / in breadcrumbs

empapado (de)	to be soaked (in) (usually milk)
emparedados	small cakes
emparedados de ternera y jambón	fried veal and ham sandwich
emperador	swordfish
empradado	a dish of codfish, beans and rice
en sazón	in season
en su tinta	food cooked in its own ink (e.g. squid)
encebollado	dish cooked with onions
enchilada	i) stuffed corn pancake seasoned with chilli ii) meat pie
enchiloso	hot, peppery, spicy
encurtido	pickled / preserved
endibia	chicory / belgian endive
endrina	sloe berry
enebro	juniper berry
eneldo	dill
enrollado	rolled
ensaimadas	sweet rolls of delicate puff pastry - traditionally shaped into spirals or snail shells
ensalada	salad
ensalada a la andaluza	tomatoes, onion, peppers, garlic and olives marinated in an oil and vinegar dressing
ensalada catalana	a lettuce, tomato, pepper and onion salad with olives and cold cuts of meat
ensalada de boquerones	a salad of soused anchovies
ensalada de chevre chaud	a salad of lettuce, green beans, mushrooms, warm goat's cheese and toast with a vinaigrette dressing
ensalada de col	coleslaw
ensalada de crudites	a lettuce, tomato, corn, carrot, cucumber and pepper salad with a vinaigrette sauce
ensalada de piperrada	a cucumber, tomato and sweet pepper salad, served with vinaigrette
ensalada de tomate	a tomato and olive salad, with a salt and oil dressing
ensalada del tiempo	seasonal salad
ensalada francesa	an endive salad with chicken, peppers, corn, pine-nuts and a red sauce dressing
ensalada italiana	a tomato, mozzarella, olives and basil salad with salt and oil

ensalada madrileña different lettuces mixed with tomatoes, anchovies, olives and a red wine vinaigrette - sliced hard-boiled eggs are used for garnish

ensalada mixta a salad with lettuce, tomatoes, onions and olives

ensalada murciana a tomato, watercress and endive salad

ensalada nicoise a salad of lettuce, tomato, peppers, green beans, tuna, boiled potatoes, eggs, anchovies and olives, served with a vinaigrette dressing

ensalada rusa a vegetable salad - generally consisting of potatoes, carrots, peas, beans, garlic and peppers coated in home-made mayonnaise

ensalada sevillana a chicory and endive, black olive and tarragon salad, served with a vinaigrette

ensalada valenciana a salad of lettuce, green peppers, oranges, onion and olives - served with a vinaigrette dressing and croutons

ensalada verde a green salad (lettuce, olives, etc) with a vinaigrette dressing

ensaladilla rusa vegetable salad in mayonnaise dressing

entrada starter/appetiser

entrecot fillet steak

entrecó fillet steak

entremeses starters / appetisers / hor d'oeuvres

entremeses variados assorted appetisers

erizo (de mar) sea urchin

escabechado pickled

escabeche (en) pickled / dish in a sweet and sour sauce

escaldums de gallina a stew of steamed chicken pieces, fried with onion, garlic, tomato, wine and slices of sobrasada - a majorcan speciality

escalfado poached

escalibada roasted pepper salad

escalivada roasted / chargrilled vegetables, usually refers to peppers (capsicums (USA)) and aubergines (egg plant (USA)) served with an olive oil and parsley dressing

escalonia shallot

escama descaled

escarchado frosted / crystallised, candied (fruit)

escarcho roach

escarola	curly endive
escolano	ling (fish), similar to whiting
escorpion	weever (fish)
escribano	bunting
escudella	a catalan chick-pea and meat stew, usually this denotes a 'hotpot' - a meal in a pot
escudella i carn d'olla	a catalan cocido
escualo	shark (spiny)
escupiñas	shell fish
esnegorri	a variety of wild mushroom
espadín	sprat
espagueti	spaghetti
espárragos (puntas de)	asparagus (tips)
espárragos amargueros	'bitter' asparagus
espárragos blancos	white asparagus stalks
espárragos montañes	calves' / lambs' tails stewed with tomatoes
espárragos trigueros	wild asparagus - a slightly bitter flavour
especialidades de la casa	specialities of the house
especialidades locales	local specialities
especias	seasoning (spice)
espetones	a term to indicate food, cooked/grilled in a 'row' or 'on a spit' - usually refers to sardines
espina	fish bone
espinaca	spinach
espinacas a la catalana	spinach cooked with oil, garlic, pine nuts, bacon bits and raisins
espinacas a la crema	creamed spinach
espineta	tuna fish
espinigada	a pie topped with small eels and spinach - a majorcan speciality
espuma (de fruta)	fruit (mousse)
espumoso	sparkling / frothy
esqueixada	raw codfish with peppers and onion
estilo	in the style of ...
estofado	stewed

estofado a la andaluza

cubed veal casseroled with a variety of vegetables in a peppercorn, cloves, garlic and cinnammon wine sauce

estofado de cordero a la andaluza
lamb sautéed with garlic, casseroled with onions and stock - a paste of garlic, pepper and mint is added before serving

estofado de lengua   braised tongue (usually pork)

estornino   mackerel

estragón   tarragon

esturión   sturgeon

exprimido   squeezed

F

faba   type of dried bean

fabada   a pork, bean and black pudding stew

fabada asturiana   a famous dish of gammon, pigs' trotters, onion, butter beans, which is simmered for hours - chorizo and morcilla are added 30 minutes before the dish is ready - a speciality of northern spain

fabes   broad beans

faisán   pheasant

fajita   skirt steak, generally marinaded and grilled

falda   flank (meat)

fardalejo   marzipan

farinatos   sausage fried and served with eggs

fasidas   similar to pizza with a pastry topping

faves   broad beans

faves a la catalana   sautéed bacon, onions and garlic added to broad beans and tomatoes, cooked with stock until tender

faves al tombet   broad beans and lettuce sautéed and casseroled with a bread, garlic, water and vinegar paste

ferraura   green beans

fesol   dried bean

fiambre
i) cold cuts of meat
ii) pâté

fideos	vermecilli / noodles
fideos a la cazuela	a dish of vermecilli, spare ribs, sausages, butifarra, ham, bacon and sofrito (usually in an onion, pepper and tomato sauce)
fideos secos	vermicelli with tomatoes, parsley, ham and onion
fideua	a dish of fine spaghetti and shellfish
figado de porco de cebolada	pork liver, marinaded in spices and herbs then sautéed with onions, garlic, wine and vinegar
filete	i) fillet (fish or meat)
	ii) escalope
filete de cadera	rump steak
filetes a la plancha	grilled pork cutlets
filetito	small slice of steak, usually served with a choice of accompaniments
filoas	sweet thin lace pancake
fino	fine
flameada	flambéed
flamenquines	deep fried rolls of sliced ham stuffed with cheese
flan	caramel pudding
flan (de caramelo)	caramel custard
flan de huevos	baked caramel custard
flan de leche	caramel custard
flan de naranja	a variation of flan de huevos - baked orange custard served in small flan moulds
flan de pascuas	cheese and egg pie
flanera	custard mould
flaos	a pastry filled with ewe's milk, cream cheese, cinnamon, sugar and ground almond
flores manchegas	thin crisp wafers of egg batter cooked on hot griddles
foie-gras	paté
fonda	similar to an inn or pub
frambuesa	raspberry
frangollo	a sweetened wheat and corn dough dessert
freír en mucho aceite	
	deep fry
frejol	type of dried bean
fresa	strawberry

fresco	fresh
freson	strawberry
frigüelo	black-eyed pea
frijole	bean
frijoles a la charra	beans cooked with pork, onion, cloves, tomatoes and chillies
frío	cold
frisuelo	dried bean
fritada de ternera	strips of veal sautéed and casseroled with bacon, onion, garlic, tomatoes and red (bell (USA)) peppers
fritangos	fried wheat and corn balls of dough
frite	young lamb, cubed and fried in oil with paprika
frite extremeña	sautéed lamb
frito	fried
frito de verduras	a vegetable stew of green peppers, onions, courgettes (zucchini (USA)) and tomatoes
fritos	fritters
fritos de espinacas	spinach fritters
frits	fried sheep's intestines
fritura malagueña	deep fried anchovies, squid and slices of larger fish
frixuelos con manzanas	
	apple crêpes
fruta	fruit
fuerte	strong
fuet	sausage / salami
fundador	spanish cognac
fundido	melted

G

gabure	i) a green vegetable soup, using all or some of the following:- green beet, spinach, mallow, sorrel and lettuce ii) a dish of pork, ham and sausages - a speciality from navarra
gachas	porridge
galianos	game hotpot (hare / rabbit / partridge)

gallego	a mild flavoured cows' milk cheese - pale yellow in colour and resembles a slightly flattened ball in appearance
galleta seca	cracker biscuit
galletas	plain cookies, biscuits
gallina	hen (stewing fowl)
gallina de guinea	guinea fowl
gallina en pepitoria	chicken in saffron sauce
gallineta	norway haddock / redfish / bluemouth
gallo	(i) type of brill / wiff / megrim (fish)
	(ii) cock/rooster
gallo de campo	farmyard chicken (corn fed)
galludo	dog fish (small shark)
galupe	grey mullet
gamba	shrimp
gambas al ajillo	prawns in garlic
gambas camarones	shrimps
gambas con gabardina	prawns fried in batter and saffron (light ale is often added to mixture)
gambas rebozadas	batter-dipped prawns
gambitas	small prawns
gamo	fallow deer
gamonedo	a smoked, mixed milk cheese from asturias - it is smoked before maturation and develops blue veins, and small holes. It is white and has a tangy taste - more picante than cabrales or roquefort
ganso (bravo)	goose (wild)
garapiñada	candied
garbanzo	chick pea
garbanzos a la madrileña	
	chickpeas sautéed with chorizo, onion, parsley and garlic in olive oil
garbure navarro	pork and vegetable soup
garneo	piper (fish) - similar to gurnard
garrafa	carafe
garrofe	beans, best used for paella
garúm	olive and anchovy dip - a speciality of catalonia
gayano	variety of wrasse (fish)
gazpacho	a cold soup, consisting of some or all of the following:- bread, oil, garlic, water, tomato, pepper and sometimes cucumber

gazpacho extremeño a cold gazpacho with tomatoes removed and raw eggs added instead

gazpacho pastor a hot terrine of various game, topped with grapes

gazpachos manchegos game hotpot (hare / rabbit / partridge) cooked with garlic and herbs

gazpachuelo fish gazpacho

gelatina jelly (fruit)

germen de trigo wheatgerm

gibeludiña a variety of mushroom

gibelurdiñas wild mushrooms

ginebra gin

ginebra con limon gin-fizz

ginebra con tónica gin and tonic

girasol sunflower

girella a sausage - speciality of the lleida region

glaseadas glazed

gobio gudgeon (fish)

gorbea a ewes' milk cheese with large holes - dark yellow rind, creamy yellow flesh in appearance with a strong aroma and flavour

gordo maize tortilla (Mex)

graixonera a mixture of sugar, milk, eggs and cinnamon

granada pomegranate

granadina grenadine (pomegranate juice)

granadina de ternera strips of ham threaded through veal cutlets, and fried with mushrooms, ham, garlic and sherry

granizado iced drink

granizado de café iced coffee

granizado de limón lemon juice and ice

grano de pimienta peppercorn

grasa fat

grasiento fatty

gratén dish with a cheese topping (usually browned)

gratinado(a) au gratin (with grated cheese)

gratinado de frutas fruits in a sweet wine sauce

grazalema a similar cheese to manchego - it is a semi-cured, well-aged ewes' milk cheese - it has a hard rind and pale yellow flesh with tiny holes

greixera de carne	a majorcan speciality - beef stewed with onions, red wine and stock - peas, beans, chorizo and tarragon are added later
greixera de macarrones	
	macaroni casseroled in milk with cheese, cinnamon and eggs
grelo	turnip top
grosellas negras	blackcurrants
grosellas rojas	redcurrants
grosellas silvestres	gooseberries
guacamole	mashed avocado served with tortilla
guajolote	turkey (Mex)
guarnición	garnish
guayaba	guava
guibelurdinas	a variety of wild mushroom
guinda	morello cherry
guindilla	small, hot chilli pepper
guirlache	almond paste / brittle
guiropa	meat and potato stew
guisado	stewed / braised
guisado de trigo	whole wheat grains casseroled with pigs feet, garbanzos, onions and tomatoes
guisante mon dada	split pea
guisantes	peas
guisantes a la española	
	peas sautéed with onion, ham and mint
guisantes a la valenciana	shelled peas sautéed with onion, garlic, wine, anise and herbs - after simmering, garlic, saffron and cumin are added
guisantes levantina	peas stewed with white wine and saffron
guisat de marisc	a mixed fish and seafood stew
guisia	tiny white pea
guiso	stew
guixado	stewed

H

habas a la catalana	broad beans cooked with bacon and spiced sausage
habas a la montañesa	thyme-flavoured broad beans
habas a la rondeña	a casserole of broad beans, onions, ham, tomatoes, paprika and hard-cooked eggs
habas con calzon	broad beans in their shells cooked with potatoes, onions and a ham bone (removed before serving) - when tender, garlic and diced ham are added
habichuela	green bean (often dried)
hamburguesa	hamburger
harina	flour
harina de maíz	cornflour
harira	chick-pea, lentil and meat soup
hashi	japanese pears
helado	ice-cream
helado confruta y nueces	
	ice-cream sundae
hervido	boiled
hervido a fuego lento	simmered
hierba buena	mint
hierba luisa	lemon verbena
hierbas	herbs
hierbas finas	mixture of herbs
higadillos salteados	sautéed chicken livers
higaditos encebollados	chicken livers with thin caramelised onions
higado	liver
higado de cordero guisado	lamb's liver ragoût
higado encebollado	liver and onions
higados de pollo	chicken livers
higo	fig
higo chumbo	prickly pear
higuera chumba	prickly pear (cactus)
hinojo	fennel
hogaza	serrano ham
hogazas	round slices of bread with spongy texture and hard crust, served with various toppings
hoja de laurel	bay leaf
hojaldre	puff pastry

hojaldre de platanos	almond and banana pastry filled with whipped cream
hojas de parra	grape leaves
hongo (negro)	a variety of wild mushroom
horchata	i) a drink of ground melon seeds and water (Mex)
	ii) almond milk - a valencian speciality
hornazo	i) golden puff pastry rolls
	ii) pie or pastry decorated with hard boiled eggs
hornazo a lo castellano	rolls of cabbage, spinach, etc stuffed with minced lamb, ham or / and pork - baked in a herb, onion and wine sauce
hornazo de salamanca	flaky pastry filled with chorizo, roast meat and chopped egg - resembles a pasty
hornazos de zamojón	rolls of ground lamb wrapped in cabbage leaves and cooked
horneado	baked/roasted
horno (al)	oven cooked
hortalizas	vegetables
hosteriá	a restaurant, often specialising in regional dishes
huanchinango	red snapper
huesillo	dried peach
huesillos	a dough with essence of orange and lemon flavourings, moulded into finger shapes and deep fried
hueso	bone
huesos de santo	little marzipan fingers
huesoso	bony
huevas (de pescada)	(fish) roe - usually served poached or fried
huevo	egg
huevos a la flamenca	baked eggs with sausage, ham and asparagus
huevos a la mallorquina	
	layers of sausage (sobrasada), fried eggs and vegetable purée baked until golden
huevos a la vasca	ramekins, filled with garlic, asparagus and peas, topped with eggs and cooked until whites set and yolks still liquid
huevos al plato a la turca	
	small cazuelas of poached eggs, surrounded by chicken livers and sautéed in sherry
huevos al roncal	eggs fried with sausages

huevos al salmorrejo poached eggs with sausages
huevos con tocino bacon and eggs
huevos duros hard boiled eggs
huevos escalfados poached eggs
huevos flamencos traditional sevillian dish - eggs fried in a
terracotta dish with cured ham, tomatoes
and green vegetables
huevos fritos fried eggs
huevos fritos a la española
eggs fried in olive oil
huevos fritos al nido slices of bread fried in olive oil. Cavities are
hollowed out of the bread and fried eggs
introduced
huevos hilados egg yolk threads candied in sugar syrup
huevos revueltos scrambled eggs
huevos serranos baked tomato halves filled with chopped
ham and topped with a fried egg and cheese

I

idiazabal a smoked ewes' milk, fresh, semi-cured and
hard cheese - it has a dark hard rind and
light yellow flesh with an excellent flavour,
the cheese is conserved in olive oil - a
speciality of the basque area
illoa a galician speciality - a mild flavoured cows'
milk cheese - pale yellow in colour and
resembles a slightly flattened ball in
appearance
infusion herbal tea
infusion de hierba
luisa lemon verbena (tea)
infusion de malva hibiscus flower (tea)
infusion de manzanilla
camomile (tea)
infusion de poleomenta
mint (tea)
infusion de tila linden flower (tea)
inglesa (a la) rare (cooked)
intxaursalsa walnut cream soup
intzaursalsa walnut cream sprinkled with cinnamon
iscas a liver dish from estremadura

J

jabalí(na)	wild boar (female)
jabalí estilo mozárabe	
	wild boar cooked with apples
jabugacitos	chorizo sausage / salami
jabugo	variety of ham from andalusia
jaiba	small hard-shelled crab
jalapeno	large, very hot chilli
jalea	jelly (fruit)
jamón	ham
jamón (en) dulce	boiled ham
jamon cocido	boiled ham
jamón de york	boiled ham
jamón ibérico de bellota	
	ham from pigs fed on acorns
jamon serrano	mountain-cured ham
japuta	i) pomfret (fish)
	ii) a variety of bream
jarabes	fruit flavoured sugar syrups
jarra	jug / carafe
jarrete de ternera a la cazuela	veal stew
jengibre	ginger
jerez	sherry
jerez amontillado	full bodied darker coloured sherry
jerez fino	pale, dry sherry
jerez oloroso	sweet sherry
jibia	cuttlefish
jicama	root vegetable - similar in taste to a raw potato or turnip (Mex)
jicamate	tomato
jícara	gourd (USA)
jijona	type of nougat
jira	picnic
jitomate	type of tomato (Mex)
judía escarlata	runner bean
judías blancas	haricot beans
judías del barco	butter beans
judías pintas	kidney beans
judías verdes	french / green beans

jugo (de fruta)	(fruit) juice
jugo de naranja	orange juice
jugo de toronja	grapefruit juice
jugoso	juicy
jurel (es)	mackerel / scad

K

kahlúa	coffee liqueur (Mex)
karraspina	a variety of wild mushroom often grilled with a garlic and parsley stuffing
kokotaxas a la donostiarra	supreme of hake cooked with peas (a rare delicacy)
kokotxas	hake cheeks / flesh sautéed with onion and garlic
kokotzas	giant tuna
koskera	i) green sauce of clams and asparagus ii) thick steaks of hake cooked in wine and garlic - peas and asparagus are added to make a green sauce

L

l'arrosseixat	a fish, potato and rice dish
lacha	anchovy, variety of sardine
lacón	i) foreknuckle of pork ii) boiled bacon
lacón con grelos	smoked or salted foreleg of pork / ham cooked with young turnip shoots - a galician speciality
lactarious delicious	a variety of wild mushroom
lagarto	lizard, usually accompanied with an almond sauce
lagópodo escocés	red grouse
laminas	slices
lamprea	lamprey

langosta	(spiny) lobster
langosta a la ibicenca	lobster served with stuffed squid
langostino	crayfish
laurel	bay leaf
lavanco	wild duck
lechal	milk fed
lechazo	lamb
lechazo asado al castellano	roast baby lamb served with a herb and wine sauce
leche	milk
leche batido	milkshake
leche (descremada)	(skimmed) milk
leche frita	cubes of thick creamy custard, covered with bread crumbs and gently fried - served hot with sugar and cinnamon
leche quemada	a light egg custard topped with caramelized sugar
leches infantiles	baby formula
lechona	young sow
lechoncillo	suckling pig
lechón	suckling pig
lechoso	milky
lechuga	lettuce
legumbres	vegetables
legumbres secas	pulses, legumes
lengua	tongue
lengua de burro	lettuce (long leaves)
lengua de cordero estallenchs	lamb's tongue cooked with onion, tomatoes, wine, herbs and parsley - dish is garnished with capers and slices of chorizo. Usually served with sautéed potatoes
lenguado	sole
lenguados a la riojana	fillets of sole served with sautéed red and hot peppers and garlic strips in oil
lenguados al graten español	sole baked with shallots, mushrooms and parsley and a covering of bread-crumbs
lentejas	lentils
leon	a cows' milk cheese - well aged, it is crumbly, strong in taste and keeps well. It has a brown rind and yellow flesh

levadura	yeast cake
liadillos sevillanos	stuffed (mince meat, ham, bacon, parsley) cabbage leaves dipped in flour and egg and sautéed
licor	liqueur
licor de cerezas	cherry brandy
licuado	shake (Mex)
liebre	hare
ligado	thickened (eg sauces, etc)
lima (Mex)	lemon
lima (Sp)	lime
limanda	lemon sole
limón (Mex)	lime
limón (Sp)	lemon
limonada	lemonade
lingote	a type of dried bean
lisa	grey mullet
lisa en amarillo	saffron-coloured mullet
liviano	light
llagosta	lobster
llano	a wild mushroom which resembles ceps but is deep brown in colour
llisa	grey mullet
llisera	flat fish similar to whiff or megrim
llobarro	a type of sea bass
llom de cordet amb trinxat	lamb cooked over coals, served with puréed potatoes and cabbage
llonganissa	a majorcan sausage
llosa (a la)	food (meat / fish) seared on slabs of slate
locro de maiz	stewed corn
lombarda	red cabbage
lomo	lean loin of pork formed in a sausage shape - eaten in thin slices
lomo alto	loin cut
lomo bajo	loin cut
lomo de cerdo al estilo vasco	pork casseroled in milk - a basque favourite
lomo de orza	seasoned pork loin, fried then conserved in oil in a clay pot
lomo de porco à alentejana	marinaded pork loin, sliced and fried - served with thickened marinade

lomo embuchado	whole pork loin / seasoned and cured in sausage skins
loncha fina	thin slice (of ham)
lonchería	a place where snacks and small meals are served
longaniza	spicy, pork sausage / quite similar to the english pork sausage
lonja	slice (of ham)
lota	rockling (fish)
lubina	sea bass
lubina albufera	sea (striped) bass cooked in an almond and herb sauce
lubina con gibelurdiñas	
	sea bass served with a wild mushroom and wine sauce
lucio	pike

M

macarrones	macaroni
macedonia de frutas	fruit cocktail
macedonia de legumbres	
	mixed vegetables
machaca	shredded dried beef
macis	mace
macizo	lean (Mex)
maganos encebollados	calamari and carmelized onion
magdalenas	lemon sponge cakes
magras al estilo de aragón	
	cured ham in a tomato sauce
magras con tomate	slices of slightly fried ham dipped in tomato sauce
magro	lean
magro con tomate	cubed pork fried with tomatoes and herbs - usually served as a tapa
mahonesa	mayonnaise
mahón	a cows' milk cheese. It has a brown rind and amber in appearance with pale yellow flesh - when aged, the cheese has a strong aroma and salty flavour, and is usually formed into a rounded-off cube
maíz (de flor)	sweetcorn (popcorn)

majado	similar to picada - a puréed garlic, paprika and wine vinegar sauce
málaga	white goat's cheese - traditionally preserved in oil
mamía	ewe's milk junket
manchego	a cheese, traditionally cured in oil, made from sheeps' milk, either a pale yellow colour with a hard straw-coloured rind or it is sometimes black. Taste varies:- i) if fresh, the cheese is creamy and mild ii) semi-cured cheeses are a little tangy, well-rounded and smooth iii) at more than three months it is dry and crumbly, with a sharp taste, similar to parmesan
mandarina	tangerine
mandonguilles	meat balls
manitas de cerdo	pigs' front trotters
manojo	handful / bunch
marvos de cerdo/oveja	
	pigs'/sheeps' trotters
manteca	fat (animal) / cream (milk) / sometimes word used for butter / margarine
manteca (de cerdo)	lard
manteca de cacao / cacahuete	cocoa / peanut butter
mantecado	i) shortcake / shortbread ii) dairy ice-cream
mantecados	almond lard cakes
mantequilla	butter
manzana	apple
manzana en compota	stewed apple
manzanillas	plump olives from andalusia
mar i muntanya	a dish consisting of both fish / seafood and meat
mar i terra	chicken casseroled with lobster - a saffron, garlic, toasted almond and hazelnuts paste with grated chocolate is added to the dish before serving
mar y cel	a dish of sausage, rabbit, shrimp and angler fish

maragota	variety of wrasse (fish)
margarina	margarine
mariscos	seafood / shellfish
mariterra	chicken cooked with lobster - a catalan speciality
marmitako	a stew of tuna, onion, potato, garlic, green pepper and tomato sauce - a basque speciality
marmitako de mar	a hearty fisherman's stew
marquesote	type of cake
marrajo	mako shark
maruca	fish, similar to whiting
masa	corn dough (Mex)
masa quebrada	short pastry
matalahuva	aniseed
mató	a catalan soft, fresh, white cheese - famously used in the dessert mel y mató
mayonesa	mayonnaise
mazapán	marzipan
mazorca de maíz	corn on the cob
mechada	refers to larding or threading strips of pork fat on meat joints to help keep meat juicy
mechado	larded
mechoni	moroccan roast lamb
medallón de pescado	fishcake
media botella	half bottle
media noche	buttered ham roll, often toasted
media ración	half a ración
mediana	i) medium (when referring to fish-size) ii) larger bottle of beer
medias lunas	small half-moon shaped cinnamon-flavoured biscuits
medio asado	medium (cooked)
medio cocido	medium (cooked)
medio kilo	half a kilo (more than a pound in weight)
megrim	gallo (fish)
meilga	member of the shark family
mejillones	mussels
mejorana	marjoram
mel	honey
mel i mató	burgos cream cheese topped with honey
melaza	molasses sugar

melcocha	honey toffee
melindre	i) honey fritter
	ii) iced marzipan cake
melisa	lemon balm
melocotones al ron	peach soufflés with rum
melocotones en almíbar	
	peaches in syrup
melocotón	peach
melón	melon
melón al moscatel	melon with muscat wine
melón elche	a variety of melon - to eat from October
melón reticulado	an aromatic melon
melón tendral	a variety of melon - to eat from October
melva	frigate mackerel
membrillo	i) quince
	ii) quince sweetened with sugar into a paste
memela	type of maize tortilla
menestra	a vegetable stew, using local produce, borage, beet, spinach, asparagus, artichokes - anything seasonal
menestra a la murciana	
	braised spring vegetables - a murcian speciality
menestra de pollo	chicken and vegetable casserole
menestra tudelana	a casserole of the smallest and newest vegetables
menjar blanc	chilled almond pudding
menta (verde)	mint (spearmint)
menú de día	set menu - price usually includes 3 courses
menudencias	chicken livers
menudillos	fried chicken giblets, liver and heart with garlic, parsley, mustard and onion - hard boiled eggs are added to the pan with salsa española
menudo	tripe in:
	i) a chilli-pepper sauce
	ii) soup
menudo gitano	a tripe dish, a speciality from seville
merengue	meringue
merienda	picnic / light evening meal
merlan	whiting (fish)
merlo	variety of wrasse (fish)
merluza	hake

merluza a la gallega	hake steaks poached and served on a bed of potatoes and onions accompanied by a vinegar sauce - a galician speciality
merluza a la sidra	hake in cider - an asturian speciality
merluza a la vasca	sautéed hake steaks served with a green sauce of asparagus, green pea and clams - a basque speciality
merluza al horno	baked hake in a white wine, garlic and tomato sauce, covered with bread-crumbs
merluza asturiana	hake steaks, baked in and served with a green / red pepper and cider sauce
merluza koskera	an old castillian speciality - hake, sautéed in a mussel or clam sauce and served with peas and asparagus
merluza la vasca	fried fish cooked with peas, potatoes and garnished with asparagus tips and quartered hard-boiled eggs
mermelada	jam, marmalade
mero	i) grouper (mediterranean) ii) halibut (atlantic) iii) rock bass
mero a la valenciana	grouper fish sautéed with a wine, vinegar, saffron and parsley sauce
mero emparrillado	grilled rock bass
mescal	mescal (Mex) (type of cactus)
mesero / mesera	waiter / waitress (L/A)
mesón bodega	wine cellar
michirones	i) spicy broad beans - a speciality of murcia ii) stewed or uncooked beans - served with a salad dressing
miel	honey
miel de caña	molasses sugar
mielga	type of shark
migas	breadcrumbs (sometimes fried)
migas de encargos	small pieces of bread soaked in water or milk, fried and served with chosen accompaniment - ham, chorizo, bacon, black pudding, chocolate, grapes, peppers, etc
mijo	millet
milhojas	millefeuille
mirton	myrtle
mixta	mixed

moixerdon	dried mushroom
mojama	an aperitive of thinly sliced salt-cured dried tuna
mojarra	two-banded bream
mojarras	sole, whiting, grey and red mullet fried together in olive oil
moje manchego	a cold broth of black olives
mojete	i) a dish of sautéed potatoes combined with garlic, paprika, tomato and bay leaf - a poached egg is often added
	ii) roast vegetables (onions, peppers (capsicums (USA))) salad, covered with a roast garlic, lemon juice, cumin and vinegar dressing
mojete murciano	a salad comprising of sweet red and green (bell (USA)) peppers, sardines or cod
mojo colorado	i) a red paprika sauce with ground garlic, pepper, cumin, oil and vinegar - a canary island speciality
	ii) boiled fish with chilli and paprika
mojo palmero	boiled fish served with a sauce
mojo verde	boiled fish cooked with coriander
moka	mocha (coffee)
mola	sunfish
molde (en)	food served in a mould-shape
mole(s) verde	thick paste of peppers, chillies, tomatoes, spices, garlic and chocolate - used for seasoning (Mex)
molla	lean (meat), flesh (fruit)
mollejas al oloroso	sweetbreads cooked in sherry
mollejas lechecillas	calves' / lambs' sweetbreads
mollejitas	sweetbread
mollete	soft tasty bread roll
mondongo	tripe
mondongo gitano	tripe cooked with dried red (bell USA) peppers and chickpeas
mongates	white beans
mongetas	beans
monjete	dried bean
montadito	small bread roll with filling, or a small sandwich, or an open sandwich - all usually toasted

montadito (de)	lightly toasted sandwich with a variety of toppings, eg ham, pork, anchovies, etc - similar to tapas
montilla	a sherry-like wine
moraga	a term to indicate food, cooked in a 'row' or 'on a spit'
moragas de sardinas	fresh anchovies / sardines cooked on a spit
morapio	red wine
moras	blackberries
morchela esculenta	a variety of wild mushroom
morcilla	similar to english black pudding (blood sausage (USA)). Most commonly sliced and fried or added to stews and other dishes - in the aragon area rice and pine nuts are added
morcilla blanca	pale, lightly seasoned chicken and fat-bacon sausage
morcillo	fore knuckle
morcillo al horno	beef stew
morcón	a rich-blood sausage filled with whole-grain rice
morella	a small, mild goats' cheese
morena	moray eel
moros y christianos	black beans and rice cooked with onions, peppers and tomatoes
morrillo	fleshy part of the neck (fish)
morteruelo	meat conserve - from the la mancha area often served as paté
moscatel	sweet malaga grape
mostachones	crispy pine nut biscuits
mostachón	macaroon, can be dipped in coffee or hot chocolate
mostaza	i) mustard
	ii) variety of mushroom
mostaza en grano	grain mustard
mosto	grape juice
mote	boiled, salted maize
mouflon	wild sheep
muchirones	broad beans in a spicy sauce
mújol	type of (grey) mullet
mulatas	ingredients of dish soaked in chocolate

música	a dessert plate of raisins, almonds and dried fruit - usually served with a glass of muscatel - a catalan speciality
muslo de pollo	chicken leg
musola	member of the shark family
muy seco	very dry

N

nabo	turnip
ñame	yam
naranja (sanguina)	(blood) orange
naranjada	orangeade
nata (batida)	(whipped) cream
natillas	(egg) custard
natural (a la)	plain
navajas	razor clams
navizas	young turnip tops
nécora	small fiddler crab, usually served as a tapa in paprika sauce
néora	spiny crab
nido	'nest' e.g. meringue or straw potatoes
níscalo	a variety of wild mushroom
níspero	medlar or loquat (fruit)
nízcanos	wild mushrooms
no incluido	not included (e.g. drinks)
no muy pasado	underdone
nopalitos	young cactus shoots (Mex)
ñora	small, dried sweet pepper
nueces	walnuts
nueces americanas	pecans
nueces de nogal	walnuts
nueces variadas	assorted nuts
nuez	nut, walnut
nuez moscada	nutmeg (powder)
nuris	small cakes
nyoras	dried sweet peppers

O

oblada	bream
oca	baby goose
oca amb peres	roast goose cooked with pears - a catalan speciality
ojo	a mexican pastry - flaky on the outside, sponge-like in the middle
olla	i) a dish of white beans, beef and bacon ii) cast iron stewing pot
olla gitana	green beans, chickpeas, pumpkin and pears simmered with fried onions, tomatoes with a crushed garlic and almond mixture added before serving
olla podrida	there are numerous varieties of this slowly cooked dish - can include any meats, any game, and any vegetables
oloraso	type of sherry
olote	corncob (Mex)
oporto	port
orduña	a very strong sheeps' milk cheese - a dark yellow skin with pale yellow flesh
orégano	oregano
orejón	dried apricot
oricios	variety of sea urchin, eaten raw or steamed with lemon juice or a spicy sauce
oronjas	a variety of wild mushroom
oropesa	a strong yellow sheeps' milk cheese, similar to manchego but with tiny holes
orperdiz a la cazuela	stewed partridge
ortigas	nettles
orujo	eau de vie (made from the dregs of grapes)
orza	earthenware dish / jar
ostion(es)	oyster(s)
ostra	oyster

P

pa - noli	a type of pastry
pa amb tomaquet	bread covered in olive oil and spread with ripe tomato

pa i all	bread is toasted, rubbed with garlic and skewered to dip into the finest olive oil
pa torrat	thick slices of bread with tomato, olive oil and a variety of toppings eg anchovies, cheese, ham, etc
pacharán	red liquer made with aniseed and sloes, the fruit of the blackthorn
paella	there are many versions of this dish - but the most popular tend to include chicken, shellfish, lobster, clams, mussels (winkles and cockles if available), peas, beans, garlic and saffron. Rice is added to absorb the liquid, cooked and served immediately
paella a la valenciana	a rice dish of chicken, shellfish, pork, ham, sausage, onions, peppers, peas and saffron
paella alicantina	a traditional rice dish which contains no seafood, only chicken and rabbit
paella catalana	saffron rice with squid, spicy pork, sausages, tomato, peas and chilli pepper
paella de caza	paella cooked with game as ingredient
paella marinera	saffron rice with fish and seafood
paella valenciana	saffron rice with chicken, squid, mussels, shrimp, prawns, tomato, peas, garlic and chilli pepper - the traditional paella
paella zamorana	saffron rice with ham, pigs' trotters, pork loin and chilli pepper
pajita	straw
paleta	flavoured ice-lolly (Mex)
paletilla	i) shoulder (pork)
	ii) shoulder and shank (usually of lamb)
palillos (chinos)	toothpicks (chopsticks)
palitos de queso	cheese sticks / straws
palmito	palm heart
palo de nata	éclair
paloma	squab, pigeon, dove
palometa	pompano (fish) - similar to bonito
palometa negra	black pomfret (fish)
palometón	pompano (fish) - similar to bonito
palomitas (de maíz)	popcorn
pam amb tomàquet	juicy ripe tomatoes and garlic rubbed on slices of crusty bread - olive oil and a little salt is then drizzled onto it - a catalan speciality

pan	bread
pan candeal	slightly coarse grained round loaf
pan de bizcocho	sponge cake
pan de centeno	rye bread
pan de higos	fig log - best thinly sliced and eaten with coffee
pan de trigo integral	
	whole wheat bread
pan dulce	sweet bread (Mex)
pan rallado	breadcrumbs
pan tostado	toast
panades de peix	fish pies
panadons amb espinacs	
	catalan spinach pasties
panceta	streaky bacon
panchineta	either a puff or short pastry almond tart
panecillo	i) bread roll
	ii) muffin
panellets	almond and pine seed sweets
papas	potatoes
papas aliñás	sliced potatoes and boiled eggs with vegetable garnish and a vinegar and oil dressing (tapa)
papas arrugadas	potatoes boiled in their jackets, often in salt crystals
papilla	baby cereal
papillote	cooked 'in-paper'
paraguaya	type of peach
pardete	grey mullet
pardillo	roach
parellada	a paella with no bones - a catalan speciality
pargo	bream
parilla (a la)	grilled
parillada	mixed grill
pasada por agua	boiled
pasapolas	starters
pasas (de lorinto)	raisins
pasas de esmirna	sultanas
pasiego	cows' and ewes' milk cheese with a mild white firm, creamy consistency - a milder version of the cabrales-type blue cheese - a speciality of cantabria
pasta brisa	shortcrust pastry

pasta de anchoas	anchovy paste
pasta medio hojaldrada	
	shortcrust pastry
pasta quebrada	flaky pastry
pastaflora	sponge cake
pastas	biscuits / cookies (USA)
pastel	i) mousse
	ii) cake (fruit/meat)
	iii) pie / pastry
pastel con nata	gateau
pastel de carne picada con puré de patatas	cottage pie
pastel de cierva	a meat pie, made with a variety of ingredients, including veal, chorizo, hard-boiled egg, brains and minced meat, all wrapped in pastry and oven baked
pastel de queso	cheesecake
pastel de verduras	vegetable flan / tart
pastel empanada	tart / pie (meat)
pastel vasco	custard and almond tart
pastelería	a cake shop
pastelerías	pastries
pastilla de pigeon	pigeon in filo pastry - a moroccan speciality
pastora	lamb and vegetable stew
pata de mulo	a bland, white, sheeps' milk cheese - long and cylindrical in shape (also known as villalón) this cheese can be salted (sal) or unsalted (sin sal)
pataco	a tuna, tomato, potato, snails and sherry casserole - a crushed saffron, garlic, parsley and almond paste is added
patas	trotters (feet)
patata al horno	baked potato
patatas	potatoes
patatas a la importancia	
	sliced potatoes fried in a sauce of garlic, parsley and clams
patatas a la panadera	potatoes baked with onions and bay leaves in white wine
patatas a lo pobre	potato dish with peppers and garlic
patatas arrugadas	small potatoes boiled in their skins and served with alioli or mojo verde

patatas bravas	potatoes cubed and fried - served with a picante tomato sauce
patatas cerdeña	mashed potatoes
patatas con relleno	mashed potatoes layered with a thick sauce of onion, ham, chicken and olives
patatas fritas	chips / french fries (USA)
patatas nuevas	new potatoes
patatas tempranas	new potatoes
patatones	fried potato chunks served with a variety of dips
pato	duck / duckling
pato a la gallega	a rich duckling dish - casseroled with bacon, turnips, carrots, onions, wine, herbs, garlic and chestnuts
pato a la sevillana	duck cooked with olives
pato a la vasca	a basque speciality - duckling casseroled with white wine, onions and herbs
pato montanesa	duckling braised with tomatoes, sherry and paprika - served with button mushrooms, small onions and new potatoes
pato silvestre agridulce	
	sweet and sour wild duck
paviá	battered fish or seafood
pavo	turkey
pavo mallorquin	turkey stuffed with black cherries, apple, raisins, pine kernels and sherry - a majorcan speciality
pavo trufado	boned, stuffed turkey
peceitos	almond cookies
peces de agua dulce	freshwater fish
pecho	breast
pechuga (de pollo)	(chicken) breast
pechuga villaroy	breaded and fried chicken breast - served with a béchamel sauce
pedroches	a sheep's milk cheese, light yellow in appearance, originating from córdoba - it is sometimes kept in vats of oil and has a strong, salty, tangy taste
peixe sapo frito	monkfish marinaded with parsley, lemon juice and sautéed - a galician speciality
pejines	similar to sardines, usually flambéed at your table

peladilla	sugared almond / coated almond
pelados (mariscos)	shelled (seafood)
pelota	meat minced and spiced with garlic and cinnamon
peluda	scaldfish
pepinillos	pickles / gherkins
pepino	cucumber
pepita	seed
pepitoria	a ground almond sauce
pepitoria de gallina	chicken casseroled with hazelnuts, ham and hard boiled egg yolks
pepitorias de gallina	a fricassé of rice and chicken, a castile and león speciality
pera	pear
perca	perch
percebe	a type of sea / rock or goose barnacle
perdices estofadas	partridges, sautéed and cooked with onions, garlic, potatoes and mushrooms in a white wine sauce
perdigado	browned / part-cooked
perdiz	partridge
perdiz al modo de alcántara	partridge cooked with truffles - an estremadur speciality
peregrina	scallop
perejil	parsley
pericana	salt cod with dried red peppers and olive oil
perifollo	common chervil
perlón	gurnard
perretxicos	wild mushrooms
perrichico	a variety of wild mushroom
perrilla	a creamy semi-soft cone shaped cows' milk cheese – yellow on the outside and paler on the inside with a smooth salty, tangy flavour
pescadilla	i) whiting ii) small fish (hake)
pescaditos fritos	whitebait
pescado	fish
pescado a la marinera	fish and shellfish cooked in a tomato and white wine sauce
pescado a la vera cruzana	
	red snapper (fish) with tomatoes and pimientos
pescado con arroz	fish baked with parsley and garlic, accompanied with fried tomatoes and served on a bed of fried rice

pescado frito a la andaluza
    small fried pieces of fish, served with slices of lemon and sometimes accompanied by a tomato sauce

pescado rebozado   fish in batter

pescados a la asturiana
    fish cooked with onions, wine, grated chocolate and mushrooms

pescaíto   an andalusian speciality of fried fish

pestiños   fried golden squares of pastry, dipped into honey syrup and sprinkled with sugar

petisús   eclairs

pez   fish

pez angel   angel fish

pez cinto   scabbard fish

pez de san pedro   john dory (fish)

pez espada   swordfish / emperor fish

pez limon   amberjack (fish)

pez martillo   hammerhead shark

picada   a garlic, toasted almonds, fried bread and olive oil paste. Chocolate, nuts, spices and parsley are also often added to make the paste - a catalan sauce, generally used to flavour food while cooking - similar to sofrito and romesco sauces

picadillo   i) minced meat
    ii) strips of beef / finely chopped beef fried with onions, garlic, chilli, chayote, olives, potato, courgettes, carrots and tomatoes - peas and almonds are added before serving

picante   hot (spicy)

pichón   pigeon

pico de gallo   a mexican salad of jicama, oranges and limes - sprinkled with a spicy sauce

picota   cherry

pierna   leg

pies de rata   a variety of wild mushroom - ochre coloured

pijama   an ice cream covered flan with tinned fruit and piped cream on top

pijota   hake

pilonga (castaña)   dried chestnut

pil-pil   a piquant garlic sauce
pimentón   paprika / cayenne pepper
pimentos rellenos   stuffed peppers
pimienta (negra) (blanca)
    pepper (black) (white)
pimienta de jamaica /
  inglesa   allspice
pimiento (verde)   (green) (bell (USA)) pepper (vegetable)
pimiento chile   chili pepper
pimiento morrón   pimento / sweet pepper
pimientos a la malagueña
    a tapa of roasted peppers (capsicums (USA))
    mixed with onions and garlic in oil
pimientos a la riojana
    sweet peppers stuffed with minced meat
pimientos choriceros   sweet peppers (dried)
pimientos encarnados
    red peppers
pimientos mixtos   mixed sweet (bell (USA)) peppers
pimientos morrones   sweet red (bell (USA)) peppers
piña   pineapple
pinchitos   meat skewered, grilled and flavoured with
    cumin
pincho   a piece of bread with various toppings
pincho moruno   shish kebab
pinchos   served as hors d'oeuvres - cubes of chicken
    livers, ham, mushrooms, peppers, onions,
    pork or lamb marinaded in olive oil and
    herbs. Threaded onto skewers they are
    cooked over charcoal or grilled
piñon   pine nut
pintada   guinea fowl
pintaroja   dog fish (small shark)
pinzas   pincers
pio antequerano   an orange, cod and olive sauce
pipa   sunflower seed
piperrada vasca   a basque omelette - more similar to
    scrambled eggs with finely chopped red
    (bell (USA)) peppers and tomatoes (lean
    bacon or ham may also be added)
pipian   raw pumpkin seeds (Mex)

pipián	stew
pipirrana	i) a salt cod and green salad
	ii) a salad of small pieces of marinaded fish with green pepper, onion, tomato and olive oil
pipirranas	long green peppers, used in gazpachos and vegetable salads
pisto	a vegetable stew of green (bell (USA)) peppers, aubergines (egg plant (USA)), onions, courgettes (zucchini (USA)) and tomatoes
pisto asturiano	ham is added to a mixture of sautéed vegetables - the dish is garnished with chopped hardboiled eggs
pisto catellano	i) a mixture of a variety of sautéed seasonal vegetables and bacon, beaten eggs are added, poached or fried eggs could also be served as an accompaniment
	ii) braised peppers and aubergine, often served with roasted meats
pisto manchego	there are many variations of this dish; the la mancha speciality consists of aubergines fried in olive oil, red and green (bell (USA)) peppers, tomatoes and squash
pitso	similar to catalan samfaina - a dish of braised peppers, tomatoes, aubergine (egg plant (USA)) and courgette (zucchini (USA))
pitufo	small filled baguette
plancha (a la)	grill/griddle (grilled)
plantano	type of banana
plátano	banana
platija	plaice / flounder
plato (de)	plate (of) ......
plato de toro del día	'bull dish' of the day
plato del día	dish of the day
platos combinados	set menu
platos fríos	cold dishes
platos típicos	specialities
pochas	depending on region can mean any one of the following:
	i) dried beans
	ii) dark beans from the navarre region
	iii) tender white haricot beans
	iv) bean soup with sausage - an aragon favourite

poco hecho	underdone (rare)
polla de agua	moorhen
pollitos pequeños fritos	small pieces of chicken dredged in flour and fried in olive oil
pollo	chicken
pollo a la brasa	grilled chicken
pollo a la campurriana	chicken cooked with white wine and rice
pollo a la española	a casserole of chicken, ham, wine, herbs and pine nuts - a speciality of new castille
pollo a la extremeña	chicken casseroled with wine, honey, lemon, rosemary and onion
pollo a la vasca	fried chicken cooked in an onion, tomato and red (bell (USA)) pepper sauce - a basque speciality
pollo de granja	free range chicken
pollo en chanfaina	chicken casseroled with garlic, aubergines (egg plant (USA)), onions, peppers (capsicums (USA)), tomatoes, wine and herbs - a catalan speciality
pollo en pepitoria	fried chicken and onions cooked in a white wine stock - egg yolk, almonds and herbs are added near the end of cooking
pollo granadina	chicken cooked with wine and ham
pollo marino	a type of tuna
pollo pibil	marinaded chicken baked in banana leaves (Mex)
pollo tomatero	sautéed chicken and ham cooked in an onion, tomato and garlic sauce
polpo	squid
polvorones	i) almond sweetmeats wrapped in twists of paper - sometimes eaten with sherry ii) light and crumbly shortbread biscuits / cookies (USA)
pomelo	grapefruit (Mex)
ponche segaria	egg toddy
porción	i) slice (of cake) ii) generous portion
porra antequerana	a vegetable dip (puréed tomatoes, peppers (capsicums (USA)) and garlic in oil)
porro	leek
porrón	glass vessel used at arm's length to drink wine

porrusalda	salt cod cooked with leeks
postre	dessert
postre de bizcocho, jerez, gelatina, frutas y nata	trifle
postre de músico	a selection of nuts and dried fruits e.g. whole almonds, toasted hazelnuts, dried figs and raisins
postre de plátano	banana split
potaje	thick soup / stew / hotpot
potaje canario	a vegetable, potato and bean stew
potaje de garbanzos y espinacas a la española	a fish-based soup of dried peas, spinach and seasoning
potaje napolitano	a potato, tomato and watercress soup - served with croûtons
pote	usually denotes a 'hotpot' - meal in a pot
pote gallego	stew with beans, meat, potatoes and greens
pozole	pork and ground corn soup
presa (de carne)	piece of food (meat)
primavera	spring
pucherete	white bean soup
pucherete de parzán	a mixed stew of beans, sausage and vegetables
puchero	i) stew or cooking pot ii) denotes a 'hotpot' - meal in a pot
puchero canario	a dish of beef, yam, squash and corn
puddin de verduras	vegetable mousse
pudín	variety of crème caramel
puerco	pork (Mex)
puerro	leek
pulenta	stew
pulpetas	sautéed rolls of veal and ham casseroled with onions and sherry
pulpitos	baby octopus
pulpo	octopus
pulpo á feira	stewed octopus in paprika
pulpo gallega	sliced, stewed octopus with garlic and paprika
pulque	fermented sap of maguey cactus (Mex)
puntill(it)as	small squid - usually fried whole

puón originally made from cows' milk and aged in mountain caves, this cheese, which resembles roquefort in taste, is now produced industrially and is generally made from mixed sheeps', cows' and goats' milk. The skin is dark grey and encased in leaves

pure de lentejas lentil purée

pure de san juan kidney bean soup

purrusalda i) stewed leeks
ii) simmered salt cod with potatoes and leeks

puzol a valencian, white, fresh cheese of unfermented ewes' milk - mild in taste - meant to be eaten fresh

Q

queimada 'witches brew' - a fiery galician drink made from burning grape skins and adding lemon, sugar and coffee grains

quelites stewed green vegetables

quemado burned

quesada a sweet made from fresh cheese, honey and butter

quesadillas folded tortillas with a variety of various fillings e.g. onion, mince, coriander, cheese, tomato, avocado, etc - a mexican speciality

quesadillas de hierro cheese tarts - a canary island speciality

queso cheese

queso (de) fundido melted cheese i.e. fondue

queso ahumado smoked cheese

queso blanco white cheese

queso cremoso full fat cheese

queso de cabra goat cheese

queso rallado grated cheese

queso requesón type of cottage cheese

queso suizo swiss cheese

quesucos a cheese made from cows' and goats' milk - a smoky yellow rind and pale yellow flesh. A mildly flavoured cheese

quinto	a small bottle of beer
quisquillas	common prawns (small shrimps)

R

rabadilla de buey	rump steak
rábano (picante)	radish (horseradish)
rabas	crisply fried pieces of squid
rajas con limon	roasted chillies marinaded with onions, lime juice and oregano
rallado	shredded / grated
rana	frog
rape	angler fish / monkfish
rape a la levantina	a valencian dish of monkfish, casseroled with a medium thick sauce of onion, garlic, parsley, olive oil and saffron
rape a la malagueña	monkfish served with an almond, hazelnut and bread crumb sauce - an andalusian dish
rape gallego	monkfish casseroled with almonds and saffron
rascacio	rascasse / hog fish
raspa	brown sugar (Mex)
rata	stargazer (fish)
raya	skate, ray (fish)
rebozado	meat / fish / poultry coated in egg, and / or breadcrumbs and deep fried
recado	i) seasoning ii) a marinaded sauce of garlic, peppercorns, spices and vinegar - often served with fish - a mexican speciality
recado de bisteck	pungent water-based sauce
recau	thick vegetable broth
recomendamos	we recommend
redondo	'roundish' piece of meat
refresco	drink / soft drink - often blended fruit drinks with cold water and ice added
regañaos	pastry with sardines and a few strips of red pepper in the crust

regular	medium
rehogado	'browned'
relleno	stuffing / filling
remojo	soaking
remojón	orange salad (usually accompanies fish)
remolacha	beetroot
rémol	brill
reo	salmon trout
repollo	cabbage
requesón	soft white cheese
res	beef
reserva	aged wine
revoltillo de sobrasada	
	scrambled eggs with soft red majorcan sausage
revuelto	scrambled
revuelto de	eggs scambled with ...
ribereña	a salmon and cider dish - an asturian speciality
ribiero	a slightly sour galician wine
riñones	kidneys
riñones a la broche de inca	
	fried lamb's kidneys, skewered with lemon pieces and served with a red wine, garlic and lemon juice sauce
riñones a la cántabra	an old castillian speciality of lamb's kidneys, bacon, tomato, sausages and mushrooms - threaded onto skewers and grilled or cooked over charcoal
riñones a la vasca	cubed veal kidneys, sautéed with onions, stock, parsley, wine and breadcrumbs
riñones al jerez	kidneys braised in sherry
riñones con salsa mibar	
	kidneys fried with onions, sherry and garlic - chopped eggs are added before serving
riñones de carnero (a la señorito)	a dish of fried lamb's kidneys, cooked with onions, white wine, espagnole sauce, peas and sometimes sliced truffle and mushrooms are added
riñones ensartados	spit-roast lamb's kidneys
riñones salteados	'tossed' kidneys - sautéed with parsley, garlic and wine after marinading

riñones salteados
  magdalena   sautéed kidneys and potatoes
rin-rán   a dish of cod or sardines with peppers, tomatoes, garlic and black olives - often puréed
riojana (a la)   sweet peppers used in preparation of dish
rizos de lenguado   fillets of sole, dipped in breadcrumbs, rolled and fried
roast beef   roast beef, often served cold
róbalo   sea water bass
robellons   an ochre coloured wild mushroom
robellons a la brasa   grilled mushrooms
rodaballo   turbot
rodaja   slice (of salami, cucumber, lemon)
rollo de primavera   spring roll
rollo de ternera   veal, stuffed with ham and braised in wine
romana (a la)   breaded and fried
rombo   brill
romero   rosemary
romesco   i) dried sweet or hot red peppers
    ii) piquant peppery nut sauce, red with chillies, peppers and tomatoes - garlic, cognac and vinegar can also be added (a catalan sauce similar to sofrito and picada)
ron   rum
roncal   a sharp, salted and smoked, but mellow tasting ewes' and cows' milk cheese - hard yellow rind and flesh, full of tiny holes
rosada   ocean cat fish / wolf fish
rosado   rosé
roscas   large polo-shaped bread, rubbed with garlic, topped with smoked ham, tomato and roasted - an andalusian speciality
roscos   doughnuts
roscos de huevo   doughnut - rolls with a slight aniseed, lemon and cinnamon flavour, deep fried and dredged in sugar
rosinoc   a variety of wild mushroom
rosquilla   i) type of doughnut
    ii) biscuit
rossejat   fried rice in a fish broth, dressed with garlic sauce

rossinyols	a variety of wild mushroom - similar to chanterelle
rostit	chicken roasted and basted in lard
rovellons	thick, meaty golden yellow wild mushroom - has a slightly tarty flavour
rubio	red gurnard
ruda	rue
ruibarbo	rhubarb
rusos	small cakes
russulas	a variety of wild mushroom

S

sábalo	shad (fish)
sabroso	tasty / savoury
sacacorchos	corkscrew
saim	pork fat
sal	salt
salado	salted / salty
salbutes	small tortillas fried and layered with lettuce, sweet pepper, onion and tomato, very well seasoned - a mexican speciality
salchichas	sausages that resemble chipolatas but the filling is darker and coarser in texture. They must be cooked before eating
salchichon	salami / cured sausage
salema	bream
salmón	salmon
salmón a la plancha o papillote	salmon baked in paper
salmonete	red mullet
salmorejo	i) cold green pepper and tomato soup, most often served as a tapa
	ii) creamy custard-like partridge pâté from toledo
	iii) an andalucian variety of gazpacho - heartier than the usual version
	iv) special wine, vinegar, herbs, paprika and chilli sauce, used for cooking rabbit
	v) a sharp vinegar, water, pepper, oil and salt sauce

salmorejo deperdiz a la toledana	a dish from toledo - a creamy custard paté, served with roasted partridge breasts
salmorrejo (al)	various combinations of local sausages, eggs, ham, asparagus and mixed vegetables - a speciality from aragón
salmuera	brine
salón de té	tea shop
salpicado	peppered with
salpicón	i) shredded or finely cut
	ii) minced veal with onion, tomato, pepper, parsley and garlic
	iii) cocktail
salpicón de mariscos	seafood cocktail
salsa	sauce
salsa (en)	braised in a casserole
salsa a la andaluza	a fish sauce - consisting of tomato, red pepper, lemon juice and mayonnaise
salsa a la marinera	a fish sauce - consisting of puréed onion, garlic, tomatoes, wine, cayenne pepper and anchovies
salsa a la riojana	a mixed vegetable, meat stock and wine sauce
salsa al vino blanco	a white wine sauce - usually served with fish
salsa bolognesa	bolognaise sauce
salsa cruda	a sauce of finely chopped chillies, tomatoes, coriander leaves, onion and garlic - a little water can be added
salsa de almendras	a cooked sauce of almonds, parsley, hard boiled eggs and milk - usually accompanies fish, eggs, poultry or cold meats
salsa de apio	celery sauce
salsa de asado	gravy
salsa de tomate	ketchup
salsa española	a cooked vegetable, meat and wine stock, sieved to produce a sauce
salsa gallega	a salad dressing of garlic, paprika, cayenne, salt and pepper, often served with octopus, prawns, fish or meat
salsa historiada	a mustard vinaigrette with hard boiled eggs and parsley

salsa inglesa	worcester sauce
salsa mahonesa	mayonnaise
salsa mahonesa muselina	
	mayonnaise with egg whites added - giving a lighter, fluffier taste / appearance. Most commonly used for russian salad
salsa mahonesa verde	
	a green mayonnaise - spinach, watercress, tarragon, chervil and parsley is added to mayonnaise
salsa mostarda	a mustard vinaigrette
salsa para pescado	a fish sauce consisting of red (bell (USA)) peppers, chilli, paprika, tomatoes and salt
salsa portuguesa	a sauce of onions, tomatoes, garlic, parsley, nutmeg and mushrooms - served as a meat accompaniment
salsa romesco	there are many variations of this sauce - the most popular consists of blended peppers, pimiento, fried bread, garlic, tomatoes, almonds, oil and vinegar (usually accompanies fish)
salsa tártara	a mayonnaise sauce with hard boiled eggs, capers, gherkins and chives added - especially served with fish or cold chicken
salsa vinagreta	vinaigrette
salteadas	tossed / sautéed
salteado	sautéed
salvado	bran
salvia	sage
sama	a type of sea bass
sambubia	pineapple drink
samfaina	i) ratatouille-like vegetable mixture e.g. green (bell (USA)) peppers, onions, courgettes (zucchini (USA)) and tomatoes which can be puréed to make a sauce ii) a side dish of vegetables for meat, fish or poultry iii) a catalan version, used as a constituent for a variety of dishes. It is a half cooked mixture of tomato, pepper and aubergine
san pedro	john dory (fish)

san simón	a shiny-looking, pear-shaped cows' milk cheese which is smoked during maturation . It has a milky, smoky flavour with a pleasant tang
sanco	type of stew
sancochado	meat, yucca and plantain stew
sancocho	i) a fish stew - speciality of the canary islands ii) a stew of meat, yucca and plantain
sandía	watermelon
sandwich doble	club sandwich
sanfaina	similar to a ratatouille - roasted peppers (capsicums (USA)), onions, aubergines (egg plants (USA)), courgettes (zucchini (USA)) and garlic cooked in olive oil until soft
sangre	blood
sangría	an iced red wine, brandy, mineral water and fruit juice punch. Served with sliced oranges and other fruit and sugar
saragalla	shredded fish cooked with tomatoes, almonds, spices, chillies, capers and raisins
sarda	mackerel
sardina	sardine
sardinas en lata	tinned sardines
sardinas pequeñas	sprats
sardinas trechadas	boned and stuffed sardines
sargo	bream
sebo	suet
seco	dry / dried
seco de cabrito	goat meat stew
semillas de alcaravea	caraway
semillas de amapola	poppyseeds
semiseco	an expression, usually describing cheese - a firm texture with a mild taste – as it matures there is a sharper flavour
sémola	semolina
sepia	cuttlefish
serandell	scaldfish
serena	both semi cured and cured sheeps' milk cheese - has a mild taste with a slight bite - a vegetable coagulent is used instead of animal rennet

serrano	i) similar to grouper fish
	ii) 'mountain style'
servicio	service charge
servilleta	napkin (serviette)
sesos	brains
sesos a la catalana	calf's or lamb's brains sautéed and served with an artichoke heart and potato purée
sesos a la romano	deep fried sheep's brains
sesos en adobo	lamb's brains, marinaded in wine and served as a tapa
sesos nuecos	brains (most often, calf's or lamb's) covered in batter and deep fried
seta	wild mushroom
seta de marzo	a variety of wild mushroom
setas a la kashera	sautéed wild mushrooms
setas salteados	sautéed mushrooms
sevillana (a la)	usually denotes dish is cooked with olives
shangurro	i) large spider crabs
	ii) crab stuffed with a thick mixture of oninons, tomatoes, parsley and white wine - a basque speciality
sidra	cider
sierra	spanish mackerel (Mex)
sin pepitas / semillas	seedless
sin sal	without salt
sitake	a variety of wild mushroom
sobaos pasiegos	a sponge cake, a speciality from aragon
sobrasada	soft pork sausage, with sweet and hot peppers
sobrasada (mallorquina)	
	mild form of pink sausage, flavoured with sweet paprika powder, and is paste-like in consistency - a majorcan speciality. Sobrasada is often added to sauces
soda	soda water
sofreigt	slowly sautéed onions, tomatoes, garlic, peppers capsicums (USA)) and herbs - same as sofrito - often used as a basis for a sauce
sofrit pag'es	i) a chicken, lamb, salt pork, sausage and potato stew
	ii) potatoes and red (bell (USA)) peppers stewed in olive oil - an ibizan speciality

sofrito	a catalan fried sauce of garlic, onion, tomato and parsley - used to flavour food while cooking - similar to picada and romesco sauces
soja	soy
soldaditos de pavía	sticks of salt cod fried in crisp batter
solomillo de cerdo a la trianera	fillet of pork roasted with sherry
sopa	soup
sopa a la mallorquina	madeiran white wine, tomato and fish soup - served with toasted bread
sopa al cuarto de hora	a rich fish soup, consisting of cockles, a variety of fish, ham and vegetables. Its name is derived from the last quarter of an hour of cooking
sopa de ajo (a la madrileña)	garlic soup with fried bread, oil and paprika
sopa de albondiguillas la barcelonesa	a soup with deep-fried lamb and pork, garlic, espagnole sauce and chopped parsley meat-balls
sopa de cebolla	an onion soup served with slices of toasted bread
sopa de datiles	a mussel stew - a valencian speciality
sopa de gañan	a hearty vegetable and chicken soup
sopa de papas	a potato and onion soup with parsley and sherry
sopa de pescado	fish soup
sopa de picadillo	a soup consisting of chicken, beef and chickpeas cooked in vegetable stock, with rice or noodles - eggs and ham are also added
sopa de uvas blancas malagueña	cold grape soup
sopa de verdura	a mixed vegetable soup
sopa gaditana	a chicken-broth based soup with fried cubes of bread and ham, sherry, hard boiled eggs and parsley added - a speciality of càdiz
sopa gratinada de cebolla	french onion soup
sopa juliana	bouillon of finely shredded vegetables
sopa mezclada (escudella)	a hearty saffron coloured soup, with vegetables (potatoes, turnips, beans, etc) - rice and vermicelli is also added

sopa seca	a term used in mexico which relates to rice, pasta or tortilla dishes
sopa sevillana	tasty fish and seafood soup made with mayonnaise
sopa viña AB	sherried fish soup
sopapillas	sweet tortilla fritters - usually served drizzled with maple syrup or honey and dusted with sugar and cinnamon
sopas engañadas	a soup consisting of pepper, onion shoots in vinegar, figs and grapes
soplillos granadinos	almond meringue puffs - a speciality from granada
sorbete de fruta	fruit sorbet
soria	a lightly salted goats' milk cheese with white skin and curd
sorroputún	tuna casserole
sortija	french sand sole
su jugo (en)	pot roasted
suave	mild
suc	juice / sauce (usually from stewing)
suela	sole
suero de la leche	buttermilk
suizos	sweet rolls
suplemento sobre	extra
suquet	rock fish stewed in a thick broth and thick sofrito (a garlic, onion, tomato and parsley sauce)
surtido (de)	selection (of)
suspiros de monja	custard served with meringues and cinnamon - served hot or cold

T

tabellas	white beans
tabla variada	plate of assorted cold cuts of meat
taco	i) cube / piece (ham, cheese)
	ii) rolled up tortilla pancake (Mex)
tacos	small tortillas, doubled and fried. Variety of fillings e.g. meat, cheese, chicken or other fillings
tajada (fina)	slice / (sliver) - (beef)
tallarines	tagliatelle / noodles
tamales	meat wrapped in masa and steamed in corn husks (Mex)

tamarindo	tamarind
tambor	tiger sole
tapa	snack on a small plate - there are many different varieties of tapa
tarta	cake
tarta borrecha	cake soused in wine or liquer
tarta de almendras	almond tart
tarta de santiago	almond and cinnamon tart - served hot or cold
tarta de queso	cheesecake
tarta helada	iced cake with sponge, ice cream and nuts
tartaletas	open, small pastry cases with a variety of possible fillings, e.g. fish, meat, vegetables or cheese
tasca	beach bar
tatemado	roasted (Mex)
taza (de café)	cup (of coffee)
tazcal	maize pancake (Mex)
té (helado)	(iced) tea
técula mécula	an almond flavoured marzipan tart
tenca	tench
tenedor	fork
tentempiés	snacks
tequila	tequila
tercio	a large bottle of beer
ternasco	baby lamb roasted (traditionally on a wood fire) with salt and garlic - a speciality of aragon
ternera	i) veal
	ii) often a term used for beef as cattle are only one to two years old when slaughtered
ternera a la catalana	a catalan dish - veal casseroled with onion, garlic, pepper, parsley, tomatoes, cinnamon and wine - lemon rind is added before serving
ternera a la manchega	
	veal, seasoned with lemon juice and salt, casseroled with tomatoes, peppers (capsicums (USA)) and onions
ternera a la sevillana	
	larded veal with wine and olives
ternera al jerez	veal, sautéed with garlic and almonds and cooked with sherry and stock
ternera de ávila	veal (three - twelve months milk-fed calf)

ternera lechal	veal (three - twelve months milk-fed calf)
ternera mechada	spice-stuffed veal, pot-roasted slowly with stock, sherry and vegetables - a speciality from extremadura
tetilla	a creamy semi-soft cone-shaped cows' milk cheese - yellow on the outside and paler on the inside with a smooth salty tangy flavour
tibia de angulas	baby eels
tiburón	shark
tierno	i) tender ii) an expression, normally describing cheese - snowy white in colour, soft in texture and mellow in flavour
tigre	tiger sole
tigres	spicy stuffed mussels
tinto	red
tinto de verano	mixture of wine and casera (lemonade or sweet fizzy water) lime juice and ice added
tipo de budín dulce	blancmange
tipo roquefort	blue cheese
tiznao	strips of grilled cod cooked with pepper (capsicum (USA)), garlic, onion and tomato
tocinillo de cielo	a sweet made with egg yolk and sugar
tocino	i) salt pork ii) bacon
tocino de cielo	sweet golden-brown toffee coloured caramel-custard flan made with egg yolk
tocino entreverado / con graso	streaky bacon
tocrudo	a mixed salad of seasonal vegetables
tojunto	i) a vegetable dish of tomatoes, courgettes (zucchini (USA)), aubergine (egg plant (USA)) and peppers (capsicums (USA)) ii) a dish of rabbit, garlic, green (bell (USA)) pepper and garlic cooked in olive oil
tomalley	coral of fish
tomatada a la navarra	a tomato dish casseroled with ham, sausages and strips of veal
tomate (frotado)	(crushed) tomato
tomate concentrado	tomato paste
tomates a la jardinera	chilled tomatoes stuffed with a mayonnaise sauce of beans, peas, artichoke hearts and asparagus tips

tomatillos	green / brown tomatoes (Mex)
tomatitos	cherry tomatoes
tomillo	thyme
tónica	tonic water
torcaz	wood pigeon
tordo	variety of wrasse (fish)
tornellas	sheep's intestines are first stuffed with meat, breadcrumbs and garlic, then plaited and cooked
toronja	grapefruit
torrezno	rasher of fried bacon
torrijas	rectangles of bread dipped in wine / sherry / milk / water, covered in beaten egg and deep fried. Served with honey, sugar and cinnamon / french toast (USA)
torta	i) cake
	ii) sandwich / french roll (Mex)
	iii) unleavened flour and water bread
torta de anchoas	a bar snack or appetiser - a thick slice of country bread, rubbed with a cut tomato and covered with anchovy fillets in oil
torta de avena	oatcake
tortas	round, semi-soft cheese from cáceres
tortells	baked almond, sugar, potato and lemon filling in a rectangle of pastry - a catalan speciality
tortilla	i) firm golden omelette of egg and other ingredients e.g. potato, onion
	ii) flat corn pancake (Mex)
tortilla al sacromonte	
	a creamy white omelette traditionally made of calf's brains, chicken livers, diced ham, potatoes and peas
tortilla al salmorrejo	potato and rice omelette
tortilla capuchina	an asparagus and potato omelette
tortilla catalana	finely chopped onion omelette
tortilla coruñesa	bacon and parsley omelette - paprika is also added
tortilla de patatas	a spanish omelette of potatoes, eggs and onion
tortilla española	an omelette of tender potatoes and onions, fried in oil with eggs added
tortilla espárragos silvestre	wild asparagus omelette

tortilla murciana	an omelette of eggs, courgettes (zucchini (USA)), aubergines (egg plant (USA)) and finely chopped sweet (bell (USA)) peppers, sometimes tomatoes, peas and strips of red / green peppers (capsicums (USA)) are also added
tortillitas de camarones	
	shrimp fritters
tortitas	waffles / pancakes
tórtola	turtle dove
tortuga	turtle
tostada	sliced white bread, buttered and grilled / toasted
tostado	i) toasted (bread, almonds, etc)
	ii) roasted (coffee)
tostados	tortilla with different fillings
tostón	i) croûton
	ii) baby pig
totopos fritos	tortilla chips (Mex)
tourin de catalonia	a ham, celery and white wine soup, served with croûtons
trangurro	spider or spiny crab - a basque speciality
tresviso	originally made from cows' milk and aged in mountain caves, this cheese which resembles roquefort in taste, is now produced industrially and is generally made from mixed sheeps', cows' and goats' milk. The skin is dark grey and encased in leaves
trigo	wheat
trinxat rostit	chopped potato and cauliflower cooked with bacon
tripa	tripe
tripa a la catalana	tripe sautéed and casseroled with onions, peppers (capsicums (USA)), tomatoes and aubergines (egg-plants (USA))
troceados	cut up into bits or pieces
trompiro	a variety of wild mushroom
tronchón	a dome-shaped ewes' milk cheese - mild and light in colour
trozo	slice (of cake) / piece
trucha	trout
trucha a la asturiana	trout, dredged in flour and fried

trucha a la catalana	sautéed fresh water trout served with an onion, garlic, parsley , cumin and vinegar sauce
trucha a la navarra	trout soaked in wine, wrapped with ham or bacon, dipped in flour and fried
trucha a la zamorana	trout steamed in a court bouillon of garlic, parsley, wine and vinegar
truchas a la espagñola	trout marinaded in white wine, honey and chives and cooked slowly on oiled paper - often served with butter sauce
trufado	stuffed with truffles
trufas	truffles
tubo	glass of beer
tuco	tomato sauce
tumbet	layers of lightly fried aubergine (egg plant (USA)), potatoes, red (bell (USA)) pepper, onions and minced beef covered with sauce español
tumbret	an inverted flan of stewed aubergines (egg-plants (USA)), tomatoes, peppers (capsicums (USA)) and courgettes (zucchini (USA)) - a variety of ratatouille
tuna	prickly pear
tunedor	veal cooked in sauce - a speciality from malaga
turbante de mariscos	a platter of steamed and boiled shellfish
turrón	two types of sweet - i) made from whole almonds, in a mass of honey and sugar (sometimes chocolate is added) ii) made from ground almonds / spanish nougat
txakolí	a white wine with high acidity
txangurro	spider crab (small claws, round body and spindly legs) casserole - a basque speciality
txipirones	tiny squid
txitxardiñak	baby eels cooked with garlic
txuleta de buey	beef steak
txuleta de ternera	veal
txuritabel	roast lamb in season with a special stuffing of egg and vegetables

U

urogallo	wood-grouse
urta	fish similar to red bream / porgy (USA)
uva pasa	dried raisin
uvas (blancas/negras)	
	grapes (green/blue)

V

vaca	cow
vaca, (carne de)	beef
vacuno (carne de)	beef
vainilla	vanilla
vapor	steam
variados	mixed
vasca (a la)	green dressing of parsley, peas and garlic (usually accompanies fish)
vaso	glass
vegetariano / a	vegetarian
venado	venison (roedeer) (red deer)
veneras	scallops
ventresca	loin (fish)
verano	summer
verbena	a selection
verdolagas	purslane
verduras	green vegetables
vermut	vermouth
víbora	weever fish
vieira	scallop, often served in its shell, covered with chopped onions, parsley, bread crumbs and baked in the oven
viejas con papas arrugadas	a fish and potato dish served with a piquant dressing - a canary island speciality
vieras al horno	baked scallops
villalón	a bland, white, ewes' milk curd cheese - cylindrical in shape (also known as pata de mulo) this cheese can be salted (con sal) or without salt (sin sal)

vinagre	vinegar
vino	wine
vino añejo	vintage wine
vino blanco	white wine
vino clarete	claret (wine)
vino de aguja	slightly sparkling wine
vino de la casa	house wine
vino de mesa	table wine
vino dulce	sweet wine
vino espumoso	sparkling wine
vino generoso / de postre	
	full bodied wine
vino incluido	wine included
vino licoroso	fortified sweet wine
vino nuevo	new wine
vino rancio	mellow wine
vino rosado	rosé wine
vino seco	dry wine
vino tinto	red wine
viudo de pescado	a colombian fish stew (traditionally cooked in holes in the ground covered with hot stones)
vizcaina (a la)	a puréed sauce of ham, pork, onion, dried red (bell (USA)) peppers and egg yolks
vleja	firm fleshed white rockfish
vodka	vodka
volador	type of squid

W

whisky americano	bourbon
whisky con soda	whisky and soda
whisky escocés	scotch

X

xamfaina	similar to a ratatouille - roasted peppers (capsicums (USA)), onions, aubergines (egg plants (USA)), courgettes (zucchini (USA)) and garlic cooked in olive oil until soft

xato	tarragona salad - comprising of ground, roasted garlic and tomato paste, mixed with lettuce / endives, artichokes, celery and nuts
xolis	a sausage - speciality of the lleida region
xoriç	sausage

Y

yema	i) egg yolk
	ii) sweet made out of yolks
yogur	yoghurt

Z

zanahoria	carrot
zancarrón braseado con higo de la vera	
	roast loin of pork with braised figs
zapallo	gourd / pumpkin (LA)
zapata	a member of the bream family
zapatero(a)	hard, undercooked (vegetables)
zarza de logan	loganberry
zarza frambuesa	loganberry
zarzamora	blackberry
zarzuela	spicy fish and seafood stew
zizak	a variety of wild mushroom
zorzal	thrush
zumo	juice
zurrukutuna	a salt cod and green (bell (USA)) pepper soup

ENGLISH TO SPANISH SECTION

A

abalone (fish)	abulón
alfalfa sprouts	alfalfa
allspice	pimienta inglesa
almond	almendra
almond (sugared)	almendra garapiñada
almond brittle	crocante
anchovy	anchoa
angel fish	pez angel
angelica	angélica
angler (fish)	rape
aniseed	anís
apéritif	aperitivo
apple	manzana
apple juice	jugo / zumo de manzana
apple tart (pie)	tarta de manzana
apricot	albaricoque / damasco (LA) / chabacana (Mex)
artichoke (globe)	alcochofa
artichoke (jerusalem)	
	aguaturma
asparagus (wild)	espárragos (trigueros)
asparagus dish	esparraguera
aubergine	berenjena
avocado	aguacate

B

baby bottle	biberón
baby cereal	papilla
baby food	alimentos infantiles
baby formula milk	leches infantiles
bacon (smoked)	tocino ahumado
bacon (streaky)	tocino entreverado
bain marie	baño maría
baked	al horno / asado / horneado
baked potato	patata al horno
balm (lemon)	bálsamo
banana	plátano
banana split	postre de plátano

barbecue	barbacoa
barley	cebada
barley sugar	azúcar cande
basil	albahaca
bass	lubina (seawater) / róbalo (freshwater)
batter	pasta para rebozar
bay leaf	hoja de laurel
bean - broad	haba
bean - butter	judiá
bean - french	judiá verde
bean - haricot	judiá blanca
bean - kidney	judiá pinta / frijol / ayocote
bean - string	judiá verde
bean sprouts / shoots	
	brotes de soja
beans - baked	alubias cocidas en salsa de tomate
beef	carne de vaca (de res)
beefburger	hamburguesa
beefsteak	bistec
beer	cerveza
beer (draught)	cerveza de barril
beetroot	remolacha
bell pepper	
(red) (green)	pimiento (rojo) (verde)
berry	baya
bilberry	arándano
biscuit	galleta
bitter	amargo(a)
bitter lemon	limonada amarga
blackberry	zarzamora
blackcurrant	grosella negra
blanched	escaldado
blancmange	tipo de budín dulce
bloater	arenque ahumado
blood orange	naranja sanguina
blood sausage	morcilla
blueberry	arándano
boar (female / wild)	jabalina
boar (wild)	jabalí
bocadillo	sandwich (various fillings)
boiled	hervido
bone	hueso

borage	borraja
bottle	botella / frasco (Mex)
bottled	en botella / embotellado
bowl	tazón
brains	sesos
braised (meat)	cocido a fuego lento
bran	salvado
brandy	coñac / cognac
brandy - cherry	aguardiente de cerezas
brawn	carne de cerdo adobada
brazil nut	nuez del brasil
bread - fresh	pan del diá
bread - sliced	pan de molde
bread - sweet	pan dulce
bread - wholemeal / brown	pan integral
bread basket	cestilla / canasta del pan
bread rolls	panecillos / bollos
bread sauce	salsa bechamel con pan rallado
breadcrumbs	pan rallado
breaded (and fried)	empanado (a la romana)
breakfast	desayuno
bream	brema / sargo
bream - gilt head	dorada
bream - red sea	besugo
breast (chicken, etc)	pechuga
brill	rémol / rodaballo menor
broccoli	brécol / bróculi
brown sugar	azúcar moreno
browned	dorado
brussel sprouts	coles de bruselas
bull	toro
bunting	escribano
burdock	bardana
butter	mantequilla / manteca
buttermilk	suero de la leche

C

cabbage	col / repollo / berza
cabbage - red	col lombarda
cabbage - spring	col rizada
cabbage - white	repollo
cake	pastel / tarta / torta
calf	ternero
camomile	manzanilla
camomile tea	té de manzanilla
capers	alcaparras
capsicum (red) (green)	pimiento (rojo) (verde)
carafe	garrafa / bombona de vino
caramel	azúcar quemado
caramel custard	flan de caramelo
caraway (seeds)	semillas de alcaravea
cardamon	cardamono
cardoon	cardo
carp	carpa
carrot	zanahoria
cashew nut	anarcado
cauliflower	coliflor
cayenne pepper	pimienta de cayena
celeriac	apio nabo
celery	apio
cereal	cereal
champagne	champán / cava
chard	acelga
cheese	queso
cheese - cottage	queso requesón
cheese - goat	queso de cabra
cheese - grated	queso rallado
cheese - melted	queso fundido
cheese - smoked	queso ahumado
cheese - swiss	queso suizo
cheese - white	queso blanco
cheese cake	tarta de queso
cherry (red) (black)	cereza (roja) (negra)
cherry distilled brandy	licor de cerezas / aguardiente de cerezas
chervil	cerafolio
chestnut	castaña

chick pea	garbanzo
chicken	pollo
chicken (breast)	pechuga de pollo
chicken (grilled)	pollo a la brasa
chicken (leg)	muslo de pollo
chicken broth / stock	caldo de gallina
chicory	achicoria
chilli (red) (green)	guindilla (roja) (verde)
chilli pepper (small / hot)	
	guindilla
chine / loin (usually pink)	
	lomo
chips	patatas fritas
chives	cebolleta / cebollino
chocolate (hot)	chocolate (caldo) en taza
chocolates	bombones
chopped small / fine	cortar algo en pedazos
chops (pork)	chuletas (de cerdo)
chopsticks	palillos chinos
chowder	crema de almejas / de pescado
chump, thick part of loin	chuletón
cider	sidra
cinnamon	canela
citrus fruits	agrios cítricos
clam	almeja
claret	clarete
clove	clavo
clove of garlic	diente de ajo
club sandwich	sandwich doble
coarse grained	grano grueso
coated / wrapped	rebozado (eg with flour, egg)
cock (male bird)	gallo
cockle	berberecho
cocktail	cóctel
cocktail - seafood	salpicón de mariscos
cocoa	cacao
coconut	coco
cod (salt)	bacalao (seco)
coffee	café (see café in Spanish-English section)
coffee - black	café solo

coffee - decaffeinated	café descafeinado
coffee - espresso	café exprés / café expresso (Mex)
coffee - ground	café molido
coffee - instant	café instantáneo
coffee - with milk	café con leche
coffee bean	grano de café
coffee pot	cafetera
coffee spoon	cucharilla de café
coffee with cream	café con crema
coffee with milk	café con leche
cognac	coñac
cold	frío / fría
cold cuts	fiambres frías / carnes frías (Mex)
coleslaw	ensalada de col
compote	compota
condensed milk	leche evaporada
conger eel	congrio
cookies	pastas
coriander	cilantro
cork	corcho / tapón
corn	maíz
corn cob	mazorca de maíz
cornflakes	copos de maíz
cornflour	farina de maíz
cornish pasty	empanadilla de carne picada y verduras
cos lettuce	lechuga romana
cottage cheese	requesón
cottage pie	pastel de carne picada con puré de patatas
courgette	calabacín
couscous	alcuzuz
cow	vaca
crab	cangrejo (de mar)
crab - spider / spiny	centolla / trangurro / changurro
cracker biscuit	galleta seca
cranberry	arándano
crayfish - freshwater	cangrejo de río / langostinos / cigalas
cream - double	nata (para montar)
cream - lightly whipped	
	crema batida
cream - sour	nata agria
cream - whipped	nata montado
crêpes	crepe

crisp / crunchy	crujiente
crisp bread	biscote
crisps	patatas fritas (de churrería) (de bolsa)
croquettes	croquetas
crumb	miga / migaja
crunchy / crusty / crisp	crujiente
crystallised fruit	frutas confitadas
cubed	cortado en dados
cucumber	pepino
cumin	cominos
cup (of tea)	taza (de té)
curd	cuajada
currants - dried	pasas de lorinto
curry	cari
custard	natillas
custard apple	chirimoya
cutlery	cubiertos / cubertería
cutlet	chuleta
cuttle fish	jibia / sepia

D

dab (fish)	acedía
dairy products	productos lácteos
damson	damasco
dandelion	diente de león
danish pastry	brioche danés
dates	dátiles
decanter	jarra
deep fry	freír en mucho aceite
deer	ciervo
deer - red	ciervo común / corzo
dessert	postre
dessertspoon	cuchara de postre
dill	eneldo
dinner	cena
dish of the day	plato del día
dog fish	cazón / perro marino / lija
dough (bread) (pastry)	masa, pasta

doughnut	rosquilla / roscos
draught beer	cerveza de barril
draught lager	cerveza dorada / ligera
dried fruit	fruta seca
drink	bebida / copita
drink included	bebida incluido
drumstick / thigh	pata
dry (very)	(muy) seco
dublin bay prawns	cigalas
duck	pato
duck (wild)	lavanco
duckling	patito
dumpling	bola de masa hervida

E

éclair	palo de nata
eel (conger)	anguila (de mar)
egg	huevo / blanquillo (Mex)
egg - boiled	huevo pasado por agua / tibio (Mex)
egg - fried	huevo frito / estrellado (Mex)
egg - hard-boiled	huevo duro
egg - poached	huevo escalfado
egg - scrambled	huevo revuelto / perico
egg - sunny side up	huevo al plato
egg cup	huevera
egg custard	natillas
egg plant / aubergine	
	berenjena
elderberry	baya del saúco
elver	angula
endive	endibia / escarola
entrée	entremés
expresso coffee	café exprés
extra charge	suplemento

F

faggot	albondiguilla
fat	manteca / graso
fat-free	sin grasas
fennel	hinojo
fig	higo
fillet steak	filete
first course	primo plato
fish	pez / pescado
fish bone	espina
fish cake	medallón / croqueta de pescado (y patata)
fish finger	palito de pescado
fish knife	cuchillo de pescado
fish stew	zarzuela / cazuela de mariscos
fizzy	gaseoso / con gas / espumoso (wine)
flaky pastry	hojaldre
flounder	platija
flour	harina
food	comida / alimento
foreign (drinks, etc)	extranjero
fork	tenedor
fowl	aves de corral / gallina
free range chicken	pollo de granja
french bean	judía verde
french dressing	vinagreta
french fries	patatas fritas
fresh	fresco
fresh water	de agua dulce
fried	frito
fritter	buñuelo
frogs legs	ancas de rana
frothy	espumoso / con mucho espumo
fruit	fruta
fruit cake	bizcocho
fruit cocktail	cóctel de frutas
fruit flan	tarta de fruta
fruit juice	zumo / jugo de fruta
fruit salad	macedonia de frutas
fudge	dulce hecho con azúcar, leche y mantequilla
full bodied	con cuerpo
fungus	hongo

G

gallo (fish)	megrim
game	caza
gammon	jamón ahumado / curado
garlic (clove)	(un diente de) ajo
garlic soup	sopa de ajo
garnish	guarnición
gateau	pastel con nata
gherkin	pepinillo
giblets	menudillos
gin and tonic	gin tonic (schweppes)
ginger	jengibre
gingerbread	galleta de jengibre
glass	vaso
glass of beer	tubo / caña
glass of wine	copa
globe artichoke	alcahofa
goat (kid)	cabra (cabrito)
goose	barnada
goose - greylag	ánsar á común
goose (wild)	ganso (bravo)
gooseberry	grosella silvestre
gourd	calabaza
grape (green / black)	uva (blanca / negra)
grapefruit	pomelo / toronja (Mex)
grated	rallado
gravy	salsa de asado
green beans	judías verdes / ejotes (Mex)
green corn	elotes (Mex)
green leaves	verduras
green pepper	pimiento verde
greengage	ciruela claudia
grey mullet	mújol
griddle	plancha
grilled	asado a la parrilla / a la brasa
grinder	molinillo
grouper (fish)	mero (del mediterráneo)
grouse	urogallo
guava	guayaba / arasá (LA)
gudgeon (fish)	gobio
guinea fowl	gallina de guinea
gurnard (red)	arete / cuco rubio

H

haddock	abadejo
hake	merluza
half bottle	media botella
halibut	mero
ham	jamón
ham - boiled	jamón / cocido / en dulce / de York
ham - parma / cured	jamón serrano
hard (boiled)	duro
hard / undercooked (vegetables)	zapatero(a)
hare	liebre
haricot bean	alubia
haunch	anca
hazelnut	avellana
hen / fowl	gallina
herb tea	infusión de hierbas
herbs	hierbas
herring	arenque (ahumada)
home cooking	comida casera
honey	miel
honeycomb	panal
hors d'oeuvres	entremeses
horseradish	rábano picante
hot (spicy)	caliente (picante)
house wine	vino de la casa

I

ice cream	helado
ice cream cornet	cucurucho
ice cube	cubito de hielo

J

jam	mermelada
jellied	gelatina
jelly (fruit)	jalea / gelatina
jerusalem artichoke	aguaturma
john dory	san pedro
jugged (hare)	estofado de (liebre)
juice	zumo / jugo
juicy	jugaso / acuoso
juniper	enebro

K

kale	(col) rizada
kebab	pincho moruno / brocheta
ketchup	salsa de tomate / ketchup
kid goat	cabrito
kidney bean	judía pinta / frijol
kidneys	riñones
knife	cuchillo
knuckle	hueso
kohlrabi	colinabo

L

lager	cerveza dorada / ligera
lamb	cordero
lamb (young)	lechal
lamprey	lampreas
lard	manteca (de cerdo)
lark	alondra
lean / thin (meat)	molla / magro / macizo (Mex)
leek	puerro
leg (of chicken)	muslo
leg (of lamb)	pierna
lemon	limón / lima (Mex)

lemon balm	melisa
lemon juice and ice	granizado de limón
lemon soda (USA)	lemonade
lemon squash - non-fizzy	
	limonada
lemonade - fizzy	lemonade
lentils (yellow)	lentejas
lettuce	lechuga
light ale	cerveza clara
light, dry white wine	
	chacoli (from the basque region)
lightly salted	poco sal
lime	lima / limón (Mex)
limpet	lapa
liqueur	licor
liquorice	regaliz
liver	higado
loaf of bread	barra de pan
lobster (spiny)	bogavante (langosta)
local dishes	espacialidades locales
loganberry	zarza frambuesa / zarza de logan
loin (beef)	solomillo
loin / chine (usually pink)	
	lomo
low-fat (yoghurt)	descremado / desnatado
lunch	almuerzo
lychee	lichi

M

macaroon	mostachón
maccaroni	macarrones
maccaroni cheese	macarrones al gratén
mace	macis
mackerel	caballa / sierra (Mex)
main course	plato fuerte
margarine	margarina
marinaded	adobado

medium - dry	semi seco
mellow (wine)	añejo
melon	melón
meringue	merengue
mild ale	cerveza ligera
milk	leche
milk - cold	leche friá
milk - condensed	leche evaporada
milk - hot	leche caliente
milk - skimmed	leche descremada
milkshake	licuado
millet	mijo
mince-meat	carne molida / picada
mineral water	agua mineral
mint	menta / hierba buena
mint tea	té de menta / té de hierba buena (Mex)
mixed	mixta
mixed grill (meat) (fish)	
	parillada de (carne) (pescado)
mixed vegetables	macedonia de legumbres
mixture of herbs	hierbas finas
molasses / treacle	melaza
monkfish	rape
moorhen	polla de agua
morello cherry	guinda
muffin	bollo bizcocho / panecillo
mulberry	mora
mulled wine	vino caliente con especías
mushrooms	champiñones / hongos / setas
mushrooms - boletus	
	boleto
mushrooms - wild	boletus / cirecens / gibelurdiñas /robellons / sitake, etc
mussels	mejillones
mustard	mostaza
mutton	carnero
myrtle	arrayán / mirto

N

napkin	servilleta
nasturtium	capuchina
neck	cuello
nectarine	nectarina
nettle	ortiga
non-alcoholic drink	bebida sin alcohol
noodles	fideos
nut	nuez
nutmeg	nuez moscada

O

oat cake	torta de avena
oatmeal	harina de avena / copos de avena
oats	avena
octopus (baby)	pulpo (pulpitos)
offal	asaduras / menudos
oil	aceite
olives	aceitunas
omelette	tortilla francesa / omelet (Mex)
omelette - spanish	tortilla paisana
one course	plato combinada
onions	cebollas
onions (cooked with)	
	encebollado
orange	naranja
orange juice	zumo / jugo de naranja
orangeade	naranjada
oregano	orégano
ortolan bunting	escribano hortelano
ox	buey
oyster plant / salsify	salsifí
oyster restaurant	ostreriá
oysters	ostras / ostiones (Mex)

P

palomitas	popcorn
pancake	crepe
papaya	papaya
paprika	pimentón
parsley	perejil
parsnip	chirivía
partridge (young)	perdiz (perdigón)
passion-fruit	maracuyá
pasta	pasta
pastry	pasteles / pastas
pasty	empanadilla
pâte	paté / foie gras
peach	durazno / melocotón
peanuts	cacahuetes / cachuates (Mex)
pear	pera
pearl barley	cebada perlada
peas	guisantes / chícharos (Mex)
peas - split	guisantes secos
peel / rind	piel / corteza
pepper (black)	pimienta (negra)
pepper / capsicum (red) (green)	pimienta (roja) (verde)
pepper mill	molinillo de pimienta
peppercorn	grano de pimienta
peppermint	hierbabuena menta
peppery	con mucha pimienta
perch	perca
pheasant	faisán
pickled	escabechado / en escabeche
pickles	pepinillos / encurtidos
pie / tart (meat)	pastel empanada
piece	trozo
pig - baby	cochinillo lechón
pigeon	pichón
pike	lucio
pimento	pimiento morrón
pine-nut biscuits	mostachones
pine-nuts	piñones

pineapple	ananás / piña
pink / rosy	rosa
pistachio	pistacho
plaice	platija
plate	plato
plum	ciruela
plum pudding	budín de pasas
poached	escalfado
pomegranate	granada
popcorn	maíz de flor / alborotos
poppy seed	semilla de amapola
pork	cerdo / puerco (Mex)
pork pie	empanada de carne de cerdo
port	oporto
portion	ración
potato crisps	patatas fritas (de churrería) (de bolsa)
potato salad	ensaladilla (rusa)
potatoes	papas / patatas
potatoes - boiled / steamed	patatas al vapor
potatoes - chips	patatas fritas
potatoes - creamed	puré de patatas
potatoes - jacket	patata cocida / asada
potatoes - mashed	puré de patatas
potatoes - matchstick	potatas pajas
potatoes - new	patatas nuevas / tempranas
potatoes - steamed/boiled	patatas al vapor
poultry	pollos
prawns (common)	quisquillas
prawns (large)	gambas
prickly pear	higo chumbo /tuno
prune	ciruela pasa
pudding	budín
puff pastry (fine layers)	milhojas
pumpkin	calabaza
purée	puré

Q

quails	codornices
quarter piece / portion	ración

queen scallop	vieira
quince	membrillo

R

rabbit	conejo
rabbit (wild)	conejo de monte
radish	rábano
raisins	pasas / uvas pasas
rapeseed	semilla de colza
rare (underdone) (steak)	
	poco hecho
rare (very)	casi crudo / a la inglesa
rarebit	tostada de queso
rascasse	escórpora
rasher	loncha
raspberry	frambuesa
raw / uncooked	crudo
red	roja
red cabbage	berza lombarda
red deer	ciervo común
red grouse	lagópodo escocés
red gurnard	rubio
red mullet	salmonete / barbo de mar
red pepper / capsicum	pimiento rojo
red snapper	huachinango (Mex)
red tomato	jitomate (Mex)
redcurrant	grosella
rhubarb	ruibarbo
rib	costilla
rib chop (beef)	costilla
rib chop (pork / lamb)	
	chuleta
rib eye steak	entrecot
rice - plain white	arroz blanco
rice - brown	arroz integral
rice - white	arroz blanco
rice pudding	arroz con leche
rind / peel	corteza / piel
ripe	en sazón / añejo

rissole	croqueta
roach	escarcho / pardillo
roast beef	rosbif
roasted	asado / horneado / tatemado (Mex)
rockfish	cabrilla (Mex)
rocks (on the)	con hielo
roe (fish eggs)	hueva
roe deer	corzo
roll	panecillo / bolillo (Mex)
roly-poly (pudding)	brazo de gitano
rosé / pink	rosado
rosemary	romero
rudd (fish)	pardilla
rue	ruda
rum	rhum / aguardiente de caña
rum baba	borracho
rump steak	filete de cadera / rabadilla de buey
runner bean	judía escarlata
runny, moist texture	blando
rye	centeno
rye bread	pan de centeno

S

saddle / hindquarter	cuarto trasero
saffron	azafrán
sage	salvia
salad	ensalada
salad - green	ensalada verde
salad - mixed	ensalada mixta
salad - spring	ensalada primavera
salad - vegetable	ensaladilla rusa
salami	salchichón
salmon	salmón
salmon trout	trucha asalmonada
salsify / oyster plant	salsifí
salt	sal
salt beef	cecina
salt cod	bacalao
salt pork	tocino
salted	salado /acecinado
salty	salado

sandwich	
(on french bread)	bocadillo / torta (Mex)
sardines	sardinas
sauce	salsa
saucer	platillo
sausage	salchicha / chorizo / embutido
sautéed	salteado
savoury	sabroso
scabbard fish	pez cinto
scallops	escalope
scallops (queen)	
(shellfish)	vieiras / veneras
scampi	cigalas empanadas / rebozadas
scrambled eggs	huevos revueltos
sea bass	lubina / mero / pargo (Mex)
sea bream	besugo
seafood	pescados y mariscos
seafood restaurant	marisquería
seafood stew	cazuela de mariscos
seasoned	condimentado
seasoning	sazón
seaweed / kelp	alga
seed	pepita
seedless	sin pepitas / semillas
selection of	surtido (de)
service included	servicio incluido
sesame seeds	sésamo
set menu	comida corrida / platos combinados
shallot	chalote
shandy	clara / champán andaluz
shark	tiburón / cailón
shark (hammerhead)	pez martillo
shark (spiny)	escualo
shell	concha
shellfish	mariscos
sherry	jerez
sherry - full-bodied	jerez amontillado
sherry - pale / dry	jerez fino
sherry - sweet	jerez oloroso
shortbread / shortcake	mantecada
shortcrust pastry	pasta brisa / pasta medio hojaldrada
shoulder (meat)	espalda / paletilla

shredded (vegetable)	
	rallado
shrimp	gamba / quisquilla / camarón (Mex)
simmered	cocido / hervido a fuego lento
sirloin	solomillo
skate	raya
skewer	brocheta
slice (of bread)	rebanada (de pan) / raja
sliver / thin slice	tajada fina
sloe	endrina
smoked	ahumado
snack	merienda / tapa
snail	cargol / caracol / cangrejo
snapper	pargo (Mex)
snipe	agachadiza
snook (fish)	roballo (Mex)
soda water	sifón
soft boiled	pasada por agua
sole	lenguado
sorbet	sorbete
sorrel	acedera
soup	sopa
soup (clear)	consomé
soup (cream)	crema
soup (vegetable)	sopa juliana
soup spoon	cuchara sopera
sour / tart	agrió
soused (fish)	escabechado
soused (meat)	adobado
soya	soja
spaghetti	espaguetis / fideos
spanish mackerel	sierra (Mex)
sparkling (wine)	(vino) espumoso
spearmint	menta verde
specialities	platos típicos
spice(s) (mixed)	especia(s) (mixtas)
spicy / hot	picante
spider crab	centolla / trangurro / changurro
spinach	espinacas
spiny lobster	langosta
sponge cake	pastaflora / bizcocho

spoon / spoonful	cuchara / cucharada
sprat	sardina pequeña / espadín
spring onion	cebolleta
spring roll	rollo de primavera
squash	calabaza
squeezed	exprimido
squid	calamares
starters	primer plato
steak (beef)	bistec / filete de buey
steak and kidney pie	empanada de carne con riñones
steak grilled	bistec a la parilla
steam	vapor
steamed	cocido al vapor
stew	guisado / potaje / cazuela de mariscos (fish)
stewed	estofado
stewed apple	manzana en compota
stewing fowl	gallina
stewing steak	carne de vaca para estofar
stout (beer)	cerveza negra
straight / neat	sec
straw	pajita
strawberries	fresas
striped tuna	bonito
strong	fuerte
stuffed	relleno
sturgeon	esturión
suckling pig	cochinillo lechón
suet	sebo
sugar	azúcar
sugar beet	remolacha (azucarera)
sugar cube	cubo terrón
sugar lump	terrón de azúcar
sultana	pasa de esmirna
sun flower oil	aceite de girasol
sun flower seed	pipa
sundae (ice cream)	helado confruta y nueces
sweet	dulce
sweet and sour	agridulce
sweet corn	maíz tierno
sweet pepper	pimiento morrón
sweet potato / yam	batata camote / boniato

sweetbread	molleja
sweetbreads (calf/lamb)	
	mollejas lechecillas
sweetener	dulcificante edulcorante
swiss chard	acelgas
swiss roll	brazo de gitano
swordfish	pez espada
syrup	jarabe / almíbar

T

table	mesa
table spoon	cuchara
table wine	vino de mesa
tangerine	mandarina
tap water	agua de grifo
tarragon	estragón
tart (fruit)	tarta / pastel
tart / pie (meat)	pastel empanada
tart / sour	ácido / agrio
tartar sauce	salsa tártara
tasty	sabroso
t-bone steak (beef)	costilla de buey
tea	té
tea - camomile	té de manzanilla
tea - mint	té de menta / té de hierba buena (Mex)
tea pot	tetera
tea with lemon	té con limón
tea with milk	té con leche
tea-cup of ...	taza de ...
tea-iced	té helado
teal	cerceta común
teaspoon(ful)	cucharilla (cucharadita)
tender	tierno
tenderloin steak	filete
thigh / drumstick	pierna / pata
thin / lean meat	magro / sin grasa
thin slice	loncha fina
thyme	tomillo
toast	pan tostado
tomato	tomate / jitomate (Mex)

tongue (ox)	lengua
tonic water	tónica / schweppes
tooth pick	palillo
tope (fish)	cazón
topped / coated with	rebozado
tough	duro
tray	bandeja
treacle / molasses	melaza
trifle	postre de bizcocho, jerez, gelatina, frutas y nata
tripe	callos
trotters (pork) (sheep)	
	manos de (cerdo) (oveja)
trout	trucha
truffle	trufa
tuna (striped)	bonito
tuna (tunny)	atún
turbot	rodaballo
turkey (cock)	pavo / guajolote (Mex)
turkey (hen)	pava
turmeric	cúrcuma
turnip	nabo
two people	dos personas

U

undercooked / hard (vegetables)	zapatero (a)
underdone (rare)	crudo
urchin	erizo de mar

V

vanilla	vainilla
vanilla ice cream	helado de vainilla
veal	ternera / ternero (Mex)
veal legshank	pierna de ternera / pernil
vegetables (green)	verduras
vegetables (mixed)	legumbres

vegetarian	vegetariano (a)
venison (roe deer)	
(red deer)	venado
vermicelli	fideos
vermouth	vermut
very dry	muy sec
very rare (veg / meat)	
	casi crudo / a la inglesa
vinaigrette	salsa vinagreta
vinegar	vinagre
vinegar dressing	vinagreta
vino rancio	mellow wine
vintage wine	vino añejo
vodka	vodka

W

wafer	barquillo
wafer thin	muy fino
waffle	(tipo de) barquillo
waiter	camarero / mesero (Mex)
waitress	señorita
walnut	nuez
warm	tibio
water	agua
water (fizzy)	agua mineral con gas
water (hot)	agua caliente
water (still mineral)	agua mineral sin gas
water (tap)	agua de grifo
watercress	berro
watermelon	sandía
well done	
(cooked meat)	bien hecho / asado / cocido
wheat	trigo
wheatgerm	germen de trigo
whelk	buccino
whipped	batida
whipped cream	nata / crema batida (Mex)

white	blanco (a)
white beans	alubias
whitebait	pescaditos fritos
whiting	pescadilla
wild boar	jabalí
wild spinach	acelgas
wine - dry	vino seco
wine - house	vino de la casa
wine - included	vino incluido
wine - red	vino tinto
wine - rosé	vino resado
wine - sweet	vino espumoso
wine - vintage	vino añejo
wine - white	vino blanco
wine (dessert)	vino (dulce)
wine punch	sangría
wing	ala
winkle	bígaro
wood grouse	urogallo
wood pigeon	paloma / torcaz
woodcock	becada / chocha perdiz
wrapped / coated	rebozado

Y

yam / sweet potato	boniato
yeast cake	levadura
yoghurt	yogur

Z

zest	cáscara / corteza
zucchini / courgette	calabacín

*For the self-catering
tourist, I have includ-
ed a section of every-
day shopping phrases
that may prove useful*

In Spain shops open from 10.00 am – 2.00 pm,
reopening again between 5.00 pm and 8.00 pm.
Bakeries usually open   earlier at 8.00 am.
Hypermarkets and supermarkets stay open during lunch time hours.

In Mexico and most Latin American countries,
shops are usually open from 9.00 am – 1 pm and
from 3 pm – 7 pm, Monday to Saturday.
As in Spain department stores are open from 10
am and remain open during lunch.

USEFUL CONVERSION TABLE

| 100 g - 3.5 oz | 1/2 kg - 1.1 lb |
| 200 g - 7.0 oz | 1 kg or kilo- 2.2lbs |

ENGLISH PHRASES

2 slices of ...	dos rebanadas de ...
a jar of ...	un tarro de ...
a kilo of ...	un kilo de ...
a litre of ...	un litro de ...
a menu	una carta
a packet of ...	un paquete de ...
a piece of ...	un trozo de ...
a set menu	platos combinados / comida corrida
a tin (can) of ...	una lata de ...
a tube of ...	un tubo de ...
are there any inexpensive restaurants around here?	¿hay restaurantes no muy caros cerca de aqui?
artificial sweetener	un edulcorante
bag	una bolsa
bakers	la panadería
bank	el banco
better	mejor
big	grande
bill (the)	la cuenta
bottle opener	un destapador / un abrebottellas
butchers	la carnicería
cake shop	la pastelería
can opener	un abrelatas
can you recommend a good restaurant?	¿puede recommendarme un bien restaurante?
cheap	barato
cheaper	más barato
chemists	la farmacia
complaint	queja
confectioners	la confitería
corkscrew	un sacacorchos
cup	taza
cutlery	unos cubiertos
dairy	la lechería
delicatessen	la tienda de especialidades
department store	los grandes almacenes

do you have ...?	¿tienen ...?
do you have vegetarian dishes?	¿tiene platos vegetarianos?
dozen	docena
enough	bastante
expensive	caro
fishmongers	la pescadería
fork	tenedor
glass	vaso
grams	gramos
green grocers	la verdulería
grocery	la tienda de abarrotes
grocery shop	la tienda de comestibles
half (bottle)	media (botella)
half (kilo) (litre)	medio (kilo) (litro)
half a kilo of ...	medio kilo de ...
half dozen	media docena
hardware shop	la ferretería
health food shop	la tienda de alimentos dietéticos
heavy	pesado
how much (is it)?	¿cuánto (es)?
hundred grams	cien gramos
I asked for ...	he pedido ...
I don't like it	no me gusta
I don't understand	no entiendo
I think there is a mistake in the bill	me parale que hay un error en esta cuenta
I'd like	me gustariá / quisiera
I'd like to drink something	quisiera algo de beber
I'd like to eat something	quisiera algo de comer
I'd like to pay ...	quisiera pagar
I'd like to reserve a table for 6	quiero reservar una mesa para seis personas
I'll have ...	tomaré ...
I'm allergic to ...	soy alérgico a ...
I'm hungry ...	tengo hambre
I'm just looking	estoy sólo mirando
I'm thirsty ...	tengo sed
ice	hielo

is IVA (VAT) included in the bill?	¿está incluido el IVA?
large	grande
larger	más grande
launderette	la lavandería
less	menos
little (a)	un poco
local dishes	especialidades locales
lot (a)	mucho
many	muchos
market	el mercado
matches	cerillas
may I have some ...?	¿podría darme ...?
may I help myself?	¿puedo servirme yo mismo?
more	mas
much	mucho
napkin	servilleta
non-smoking area	la sección de no fumadores
nothing more thanks	nada más, gracias
on the patio	en el patio
outside	fuera
pastry shop	la pastelería
piece of	un trozo de
plates	platos
please	por favor
saucepan	cacerola
shops	tiendas
slice	raja
small	pequeño
smaller	más pequeño
spoon	cuchara
supermarket	el supermercado
sweets	bombones
thank you	gracias
that	eso
that one	de ése
the bill / check (USA) please	la cuenta por favor
this	esto
tin opener	abrelata

tin-foil	papel de aluminio / plata
too (much)	demasiado (mucho)
vegetable store	la verdulería
waiter / waitress	¡camarero! / ¡camarera!
we'll come at 9	vendremos a las nueve horas
what's on the menu?	
	¿que hay en la carta?
where can we get a typical spanish meal?	
	¿donde podemos encontrar comidas típicas de españa?
where do I pay?	¿dónde est á la caja?
wine	vino
wine merchant	la tienda de vinos